MEMORY MAKERS

Wedding Idea Book

Wedding
Wishes
for a
Special Couple

A wedding is a mosaic of
joyous memories...
memories that are fully realized when
they are written down and shared with others.

MEMORY
MAKERS

Wedding
Idea Book

SCRAPBOOKING IDEAS,

TIPS AND TECHNIQUES

MEMORY
MAKERS
BOOKS

DENVER, COLORADO

*We dedicate this book to all of our Memory Makers' readers whose beauti-
ful wedding scrapbooks and ideas are the inspiration on these pages.*

BOOK DIRECTORS	Michele & Ron Gerbrandt
EDITOR	MaryJo Regier
DESIGNER	Sylvie Abecassis
CRAFT DESIGNER	Pam Klassen
IDEA COORDINATOR	Pennie Stutzman
CONTRIBUTING WRITER	Anne Wilbur
CRAFT ARTIST	Erikia Ghumm
PRODUCTION	Diane Gibbs, Bren Frisch, Rudy Landry, Mark Lewis
LETTERING ARTISTS	Joy Carey, Kim Peters, Virginia Russell, Mary-Kay Tilden-Dyck
PHOTO STUDIO	Cambon Photography

ISBN 1-89212-708-3

Copyright © 2000 Memory Makers Books
12365 Huron Street, Suite 500
Denver, CO 80234
Phone 1-800-254-9124
www.memorymakersmagazine.com

Memory Makers Books is the home of *Memory Makers*®, a magazine
dedicated to educating and inspiring scrapbookers and paper artists.
To subscribe or for more information call 1-800-366-6465.

06 05 04 03   7654

Library of Congress Cataloging-in-Publication Data

Memory makers wedding idea book: scrapbooking ideas, tips, and techniques.
    p. cm.
Reprint. Originally published: Denver: Satellite Press, 1999.
    Includes bibliographical references and index.
    ISBN 1-892127-08-3
    1. Photograph albums. 2. Photographs--Conservation and restoration. 3. Scrapbooks. 4.
Weddings. I. Title: Wedding idea book. II. Memory makers.

TR465 .M48 2000
    745.594'1--dc21   00-049677

*Distributed to the trade and art markets by
F & W Publications, Inc.
4700 East Galbraith Road, Cincinnati, OH 45236
1-800-289-0963*

Contents

Illustrated
Contents

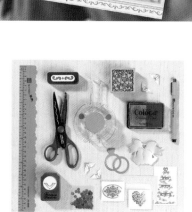

CONTEMPORARY WEDDINGS PAGE 76

CONTEMPORARY WEDDINGS PAGE 74

ENGAGEMENT PAGE 16

HERITAGE WEDDINGS PAGE 117

HONEYMOON PAGE 104

WEDDING RECEPTION PAGE 99

PHOTO KEEPSAKE PAGE 63

Jill & Randy
September 4, 1999

Introduction

There's no other moment in life like a wedding–a day built on dreams and finished with joy. The real beauty of this celebration is not fully realized until it is preserved and shared with others.

I have visited nearly 200 weddings while putting this book together. My visits have come from looking through the hundreds of wedding pages sent to us from scrapbook artists around the world. I feel as if I have sat down with each woman and looked through her personal wedding scrapbook. It's the same experience I hope you have as you look through the pages of this book.

We have gathered together many unique and beautiful page ideas. More than that, there are stories behind the pages which include helpful and clever ideas for the wedding celebration itself. There are ideas for the engagement, bridal shower, bachelor and bachelorette parties, traditional to contemporary wedding ceremonies and, of course, honeymoons. We have included historical wedding facts, unique scrapbook techniques, reproducible lettering and special galleries so you can see how some brides have woven a theme throughout their entire wedding album.

An astonishing 2.3 million brides will say "I do" this year, according to *Brides* magazine. That translates into a lot of memories and precious wedding photos. *Memory Makers® Wedding Idea Book* provides the steppingstones of encouragement and inspiration needed to get those fading memories and photos out of their boxes and into a meaningful and personal wedding scrapbook album.

Whether you are new to scrapbooking or a seasoned veteran, yesterday's bride or tomorrow's bride-to-be, there is inspiration here for everyone.

JILL AND RANDY
JOY CAREY
VISALIA, CALIFORNIA
(SEE PAGE 124)

Michele

FOUNDER OF MEMORY MAKERS® MAGAZINE

Wedding Photo Checklist

Organizing your photos and memorabilia will make the planning of your wedding album much easier. Use these lists as the basic framework for organizing your photos and memorabilia.

- ☐ Behind the Scenes Preparations
- ☐ Bride and Groom Preparation
- ☐ Bride and Flower Girl
- ☐ Groom and Ring Bearer
- ☐ Bride and Bridesmaids
- ☐ Bride and Parents
- ☐ Bride and Siblings
- ☐ Bride: Three Generations
- ☐ Bride Alone
- ☐ Groom and Groomsmen
- ☐ Groom and Parents
- ☐ Groom and Siblings
- ☐ Groom: Three Generations
- ☐ Groom Alone
- ☐ Church Exterior

- ☐ Arriving at the Church
- ☐ Processional Photos
- ☐ Bride and Father Walking Down the Aisle
- ☐ Father's Goodbye Kiss
- ☐ Readings and Music
- ☐ Candle Lighting
- ☐ Special Traditions Photos
- ☐ Exchange of Vows/Rings
- ☐ Bride and Groom's Kiss
- ☐ Recessional Photos
- ☐ Bride and Groom Leaving the Church
- ☐ Entire Bridal Party (Formal)
- ☐ Entire Bridal Party (Fun)
- ☐ Bride and Groom Together

- ☐ Bride and Groom with Grandparents
- ☐ The First Dance
- ☐ Bride and Father Dancing
- ☐ Groom and Mother Dancing
- ☐ The Toast
- ☐ Guests at Table Pictures
- ☐ Bridal Party Dancing
- ☐ Guests Dancing
- ☐ The Cake and Cake Ceremony
- ☐ The Rings
- ☐ Bouquet/Garter Tosses
- ☐ The Flowers
- ☐ The Gifts
- ☐ Signature Book and Hostess

Memorabilia Checklist

- ☐ Preparation Notes
- ☐ Bulletins
- ☐ Invitations
- ☐ Invitation Checklist
- ☐ Guest Signatures
- ☐ Handwritten Vows

- ☐ Sheet Music
- ☐ Bridal Bouquet
- ☐ Garter
- ☐ Pressed Flowers
- ☐ Napkins
- ☐ Table Confetti
- ☐ Guest Favors
- ☐ Marriage License
- ☐ Receipts
- ☐ Copy of Gift Registry
- ☐ Congratulations Cards
- ☐ Inspirational Pictures From Magazines and Books
- ☐ Map to Ceremony Location

For preservation purposes, we highly recommend the use of acid- and lignin-free albums and paper products, photo-safe adhesives, PVC-free plastics and pigment inks.

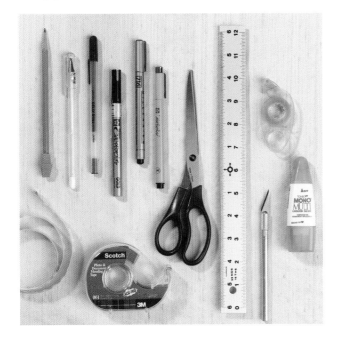

Basic Tools & Supplies

Albums & Scrapbook Pages

Page Protectors

Colored and Printed Papers

Pens and Markers

Permanent and Removable Adhesives

Ruler

Scissors

Unique Design Additions

Die Cuts

Fancy Rulers

Fancy Scissors

Journaling and Design Templates

Memorabilia Pockets

Paper Frames

Paper Trimmers/Cutters

Photo Corners

Punches

Stamps

Stickers

Guide to Beginning Your Wedding Scrapbook

Whether you are starting your personal album or creating a gift, the thought of creating the perfect wedding album may seem intimidating, even overwhelming. However, with a little pre-planning, organization and inspiration, this task will become quite manageable. Below, we have outlined the simple steps to get you started.

1 ORGANIZE PHOTOS AND MEMORABILIA

Use the checklist on page 10 as the framework for organizing your photos. As you work, jot down memories that the photos inspire. Decide also if you will incorporate your engagement, bridal shower, bachelorette party or honeymoon into your wedding album. Consider enlarging your favorite photos. Now assemble the selected photos and memorabilia to be included in the album. Their quantity and physical size will determine the size of the album and number of pages needed.

2 SELECT AN ALBUM

Albums come in three-ring binder, spiral bound, post bound or strap-bound style. The most popular and readily available sizes are 12 x 12" and 8½ x 11". Sturdy, well-constructed albums that are expandable are the best and will withstand the test of time and hundreds of viewings. Whichever album you select, make certain that it is an archival-quality environment for your photos and memorabilia.

3 SELECT A VISUAL THEME

Your wedding album's visual theme will depend on your photos and memorabilia, as well as what fits your personal style and budget. The goal is to create a wedding album that tells your story. To prevent a choppy, unplanned look, consider establishing a consistent style and color selection. The repeated use of a particular design element, such as a paper pattern, color or unique border will give the album a sense of continuity. Take your list of album layouts and some photos to the store to avoid spending money on unnecessary items.

4 CREATING LAYOUTS

Composition

A beautiful scrapbook page and album rely on balanced composition that pleases the eye. The page at right is simple yet balanced. It is easier if you don't make each page a unique work of art. Instead, consider using two-page spreads that are clean and basic. Save elaborate designs and fancy techniques for title pages and important photographs. Here are some basic concepts which will help your page composition. And remember, lay out the entire page before mounting anything.

Focal Point

A scrapbook page may contain several photos, but decide on one that is important enough to be a focal point. Give the primary photo, in this case a photo of the bride and groom, a dominant position on the page. Use the rest of the page to complement the focal point.

Creative Cropping

Creative photo cropping breaks the monotony of the square or rectangular page. Cropping can emphasize the important subject or remove busy backgrounds. Use caution when cropping, making certain you will not later regret what you have cut away. You will find many successful examples of photo cropping throughout the pages of this book.

Matting and Framing

Decorative matting and framing can help showcase your photos by focusing the viewers' attention on them. Mats can be made with colored or printed papers, fancy scissors and templates. Select colors which will complement the photos and not steal the attention.

Adding Embellishments

Once your photos and memorabilia are in place, complete the layout by adding design embellishments such as stickers, die cuts, punched shapes and more.

5 JOURNALING

A page is not complete without your own words to tell the story. Handwritten words are preferable because of their personal quality. But for the penmanship-challenged, there are countless computer fonts, lettering books and journaling templates available. We have included some lettering patterns on pages 122 and 123 to help you out. The important thing is to tell your wedding story without relying solely on your photos. Besides telling the "who, what, when and where," add stories, favorite lyrics, quotes, Scripture and poems to bring your photographic story to life.

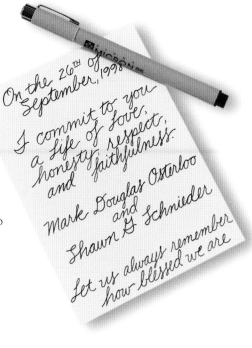

Personal Design

Successful page design is a highly personal endeavor that can be challenging,
yet fun. To prove this point, we supplied three scrapbook artists with identical photos
and scrapbook supplies. We then challenged the artists to unleash their creativity on a wedding
scrapbook page, using some of the supplies we sent. What these very different pages have in
common is a large amount of creativity, the commitment required to move from an idea
to a finished scrapbook page and plenty of inspiration to trigger your imagination.

On The Wings of Love (One)

A FEATHERED FAIRY TALE

Hand-cut paper feathers,
a ribbon banner and a real
feather accent work together
for a legendary page design.
Supplies used are vellum
(The Paper Co.), gold
metallic paper (Hygloss
Products), printed papers
(Current), ribbon (Offray),
letter stickers (Cellotak),
hand-cut feathers, border
stickers (K & Co.) and
memorabilia pocket
(3L Corp).

Cynthia Castelluccio
Carrollton, Virginia

On The Wings of Love (Two)

CREATE SIMPLE, ELEGANT PUNCH ART

A handful of punches help transform these photos into a charming yet sophisticated page design. Supplies used are vellum (The Paper Co.), printed papers (Current), lace paper (Hot Off The Press), punches (Family Treasures), stickers (Mrs. Grossman's), pressed flowers (Pressed Petals), banner template (C-Thru Ruler Co.) and quilt stencil (Heritage Handcrafts).

Marilyn Garner
San Diego, California

On The Wings of Love (Three)

STAMP A ROMANTIC DESIGN

Rubber stamps and printed papers bring out the romance in this page design. Supplies used are vellum (The Paper Co.), printed paper (Current), lace paper (Hot Off The Press), stamps (*On The Wings of Love*/Stampendous; *little rose*/Magenta; *doves*/Denami; *journaling frames*/Marks of Distinction), punches (Family Treasures) and ribbon.

Cathie Allan
St. Albert, Alberta, Canada

We're Engaged!

Scott really surprised me when he proposed! He woke me up at 9am this particular Saturday to go roller blading at Chatfield Reservoir. I couldn't understand why he was so excited to get such an early start, but little did I know of his big plan! As we were skating up a steep incline, Scott called out for me to stop. I thought something was wrong when I saw an odd, nervous look on his face. Scott started talking about our year together and how romantic it was that we were roller blading, since that was what we did on our first date. All of a sudden, he was down on one knee with the ring box open! He asked me to marry him and all I could say was, "I can't believe it!" I lunged to hug him and we just plopped down in the middle of the bike path. We spent the next few moments taking in the beautiful scenery and the turning point in our lives!

March 28th 1998

The spot where I became Scott's fiancée

Welcome to CHATFIELD STATE PARK

Engagement

"WILL YOU MARRY ME?" HE

ASKS. FOR A MOMENT

TIME STANDS STILL;

A MOMENT THAT BEGINS

A LIFETIME.

He's your true love, your soul mate, your best friend. Whether it was love at first sight or written in the stars, the love you share is confirmed in one heart-pounding proposal.

Your engagement, no doubt, had an undeniable element of surprise. With a little creative inspiration and a photo or two, you can relive this cherished moment forever on a scrapbook page.

Add photos of you as a newly engaged couple, the spot where the proposal took place and a photo of you with your new ring to freeze the moment in time. By adding mementos of that

WE'RE ENGAGED!
DANIELLE SCHLOFFMAN
LAKEWOOD, COLORADO
(SEE PAGE 124)

CONTINUED. . .

special day, a newspaper announcement, the description of his proposal, your reaction, as well as the reaction of your family and friends, you can record this memorable event for the future.

ENGAGEMENT WINDOW
KIM BONDY
ALLEN PARK, MICHIGAN
(SEE PAGE 124)

Patti's Engagement

For Patti Bowlin, an elementary school teacher, September 18, 1998, began with five hundred students, teachers and parents gathered for the opening assembly. The assembly's concept would be "teamwork."

Patti was barely awake when a special guest was announced. When the curtain rose, to Patti's surprise, there stood her boyfriend, David Million, with a dozen red roses.

"Teamwork is very important," he began. Since Patti and David would often eat lunch together at school, it didn't take long for people to realize what David was up to. He handed Patti the roses and the "oohs" and "aahs" began.

"Teamwork needs love and commitment," David continued. "And to demonstrate love, I am presenting these roses to Ms. Bowlin. I am in love with Ms. Bowlin, so I'm going to ask her to form a team with me for the rest of our lives." The crowd grew louder.

David dropped to one knee and asked Patti to marry him. The crowd erupted, drowning out Patti's response. She retrieved a microphone and repeated, "I said 'yes' to Mr. Million." And the crowd went wild.

The proposal in front of the entire school made Patti "feel like queen for a day." Students still talk about that special assembly. For David, his seven-year courtship and detailed planning all boiled down to a creative engagement that was "one in a million."

Patti Million, Tulsa, Oklahoma

Our engagement Sitting

These were the pictures we had taken to use to announce our engagement in the newspapers.

july 3, 1994

Our Engagement Sitting

CREATE SHOW-STOPPING FILMSTRIPS

Cut 4¾" wide strips of black paper;
trim to fit page when placed at an angle. Punch black paper strips with
film strip border punch (Family Treasures); adhere. Add photos. Journal with white pen.

Allie Littell, Mebane, North Carolina

WEDDING COUNTDOWN CHECKLIST

Six or more months before wedding
- ☐ *announce engagement*
- ☐ *select wedding date*
- ☐ *set budget, establish priorities*
- ☐ *determine wedding style and colors*
- ☐ *purchase wedding gown, determine tuxedo style*
- ☐ *select and reserve ceremony and reception sites*
- ☐ *select attendants*
- ☐ *compile guest list*
- ☐ *order invitations/personalized accessories*
- ☐ *reserve accommodations for out-of-town guests*
- ☐ *meet with musicians, photographer, florist, caterer, baker, officiant*
- ☐ *plan reception*

Four months before wedding
- ☐ *purchase wedding rings*
- ☐ *address invitations*
- ☐ *plan rehearsal and rehearsal dinner*
- ☐ *make honeymoon reservations*
- ☐ *obtain or renew passport, if needed*
- ☐ *arrange transportation*
- ☐ *arrange gown and attendant fittings*
- ☐ *begin writing wedding vows*
- ☐ *register for gifts*
- ☐ *determine state legal requirements for marriage*

Two months before wedding
- ☐ *mail wedding invitations*
- ☐ *finalize ceremony with officiant*
- ☐ *order wedding programs*
- ☐ *purchase attendants' gifts*
- ☐ *purchase family bride/groom gifts*
- ☐ *consult makeup and hair stylist*

One month before wedding
- ☐ *keep up with thank-you notes*
- ☐ *final attire fittings*
- ☐ *reconfirm all reservations and contracts*
- ☐ *pick up wedding gown and accessories*
- ☐ *check groom's attire for proper fit*
- ☐ *host a bridesmaids' party*
- ☐ *determine final guest count*

Two weeks before wedding
- ☐ *obtain marriage license*
- ☐ *pack for ceremony*
- ☐ *pack for honeymoon*

Autumn Engagement

TELL THE STORY IN BLACK AND WHITE

(UPPER RIGHT) Trim corners of photos and white rectangle label with corner rounder punch. Mat photos with green paper and arrange on wedding border page (Creative Memories). Accent with confetti stickers (Creative Memories).

Kimberly Macchio, Fort Worth, Texas

Will You Marry Me?

HIGHLIGHT AN OLD CLIPPING

(UPPER FAR RIGHT) Print or draw page title and ring art on white paper. Trim paper edges with decorative scissors and mount on pink background. Use templates to cut pink hearts. Layer hearts with photos and memorabilia. Adhere heart and thought stickers (Stickopotamus). Freehand draw line embellishments.

Jillyn Wells, St. George, Utah

Engagement Portrait

PRESERVE ARTICLE AND ANNOUNCEMENT

(LOWER RIGHT) Write words for page border with thin black pen. Tear white paper to mat portrait, invitation and announcement. Tear red and pink hearts and outline with black pen. Cut thin green strips for stems.

Linda Strauss, Provo, Utah

How We Met

TELL THE STORY OF HOW YOU MET

(LOWER FAR RIGHT) Using a wavy ruler and thin pen, draw a wavy line along the top edge of the page. Moving the ruler slightly down and to the left, draw a second wavy line to create the ribbon outline. Color in the ribbon. Repeat these steps to draw a ribbon along the left page edge. Draw straight lines between ribbon waves. Freehand draw hearts and leaves. Adhere heart sticker (R.A. Lang) for corner embellishment.

Liesl Walsh, Perkasie, Pennsylvania

Kimberly D. Smith & Daniel F. Macchio engaged on November 21, 1997. Denton, TX.

pictures taken at TWU.

Will you marry me?

I hope she says Yes!

young.

and in love...

amor amor amor amor amor amor amor amor

Life is a flower of which love is the honey.
—Victor Hugo

Durst, Strauss

How We Met

Lieslé · Mike

The Occasion: a singles Bible study
Where: Washington Crossing United Methodist Church
When: Friday, December 6, 1991
Who we were with: Nancy Glatfelter, Elyse Stirneman, Chuck Raphael
How did we first bump into each other? I came out of the gym to get my purse, and I saw him on a bench.

Chad and Kristen...

CHRONICLE CHILDHOOD HISTORIES

Using a ruler and white opaque pen, draw lines arour page edges. Trim photo edges with decorative scissors and triple mat with solid and printed (Paper Patch) papers. Mat paper rectangles for journaling and adhere letter stickers (Pebbles In My Pocket). Cut out bows and letters for "A Boy" and "A Girl" from printed paper (NRN Designs). Outline journaling, photo mats, bows and letters with thin pen.

Joyce chronicled the childhood histories of Chad and Kristen to lead up to the engagement.

...Engaged

TO LEAD UP TO THE ENGAGEMENT

Stamp and heat emboss title letters (Stampin' Up!) on 2¼ x 11" strip of heart paper (Northern Spy). Mat title, photos and white hearts, using striped paper (Keeping Memories Alive) for oval photo mat. Layer elements on printed navy paper (Keeping Memories Alive). Journal and outline hearts and title with thin red pen. Adhere heart sticker (Mrs. Grossman's).

Joyce Schweitzer
Greensboro, North Carolina

TRADITIONAL FINANCIAL RESPONSIBILITIES

Bride and Bride's Family
- bride's attire and accessories
- groom's wedding ring
- wedding gift for groom
- invitations and stationery
- reception costs
- ceremony costs
- photos and videography
- bridesmaids' flowers
- gifts for bridal attendants
- transportation

Groom and Groom's Family
- formal wear and accessories
- bride's engagement and wedding rings
- wedding gift for bride
- rehearsal dinner
- marriage license
- bride's bouquet
- corsages and boutonnieres
- officiant's fee
- gifts for groomsmen and ushers
- the honeymoon

How To Be a Good Wife

MAKE CHECKERBOARD TO SHOWCASE ADVICE

Use rose paper (Paper Patch) for page background. Mount 3 x 12" white strips on left and right layout edges. Adhere 1" mint squares in a checkerboard pattern. Fill white spaces with punched hearts. Cut out bride and groom illustration from printed paper (Stamping Station) and layer over printed journaling. Trim corners of photos and mats with corner rounder punch.

Carrie Davis, Everett, Washington

"How To Be A Good Wife"
By: Miss Fix's First and Second Grade Class
June, 1997

1. Take care of yourself. - Krysta
2. Give your child whatever he wants. - Joey
3. Try to be a good wife. And try not to get in fights. - Alyssa
4. Don't divorce him. - Nathan
5. Love your husband. - Taige
6. Try not to get into fights. Always love your honey. - Taylor
7. Do the dishes. - Robert
8. Be nice to each other. - Michael
9. Love your husband. Say: "Did you have a good day?" after work. - Tia
10. To love him and say "Thank you" for the nice things he does for you. - Brittany
11. Make sure that you have the right man, and if you do have the right man, stay with him. - Owen
12. Never bug your honey! - Rachelle
13. Be loving, kiss, say: "I love you." XOX - Brandon
14. Do not divorce. Care for your children. - Jason
15. Don't get mad at him. And, last but not least, be nice. - David
16. Never get a divorce. - Jeremy
17. To have a perfect child. - Caleb
18. Do not divorce. - Dillon
19. Do surprises when your husband is sick. Go out to lunch and dinner with him. Never get divorced. - Kelsey
20. Always clean things the right way. - Katie

Mini Album of Matrimonial Advice

PRESERVING TREASURED BITS OF SAGE WISDOM FOR FUTURE REFERENCE

Once an engagement is announced, everyone seems to have marriage advice to offer. Advice that makes great content for a mini album.

Keep a camera, pen and paper handy to record every little insight into the mystery of wedded life. Advice solicited by a maid of honor or best man during engagement parties, bridal showers and bachelor or bachelorette parties becomes a great gift to the bride and groom when compiled into a mini album. Another fun variation is a mini album of marital predictions for the newlyweds, complete with a photo of each "forecaster."

Stretch accordion photo album (Kolo) out flat. Adhere rectangles of rice paper (The Paper Co.) to each section. Mat photos with pink and lavender paper. Accent mat edges with white, opal, platinum paints and Crystal Stickles® (Ranger Industries); mount photos. Journal "advice" on pink and lavender paper, accenting edges as desired; mount near appropriate photos. Stamp fleur-de-lis (All Night Media) on pink and lavender paper, accent with paints as shown above. Cut out fleurs-de-lis; mount using foam spacers. Embellish pages with stickers (Mrs. Grossman's) and pressed flowers (NuCentury, Pressed Petals).

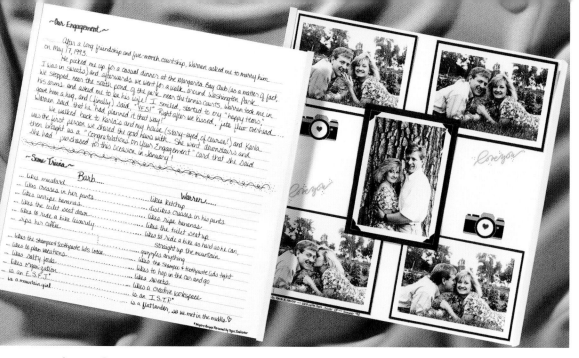

Our Engagement

CHRONICLE A ROMANTIC PROPOSAL

Use black and red pens to journal on ruled scrapbook page (Creative Memories). Mat black-and-white photos. Adhere camera, photo corner, small heart and "love you" stickers (Mrs. Grossman's).

Barb Rickford, Highlands Ranch, Colorado

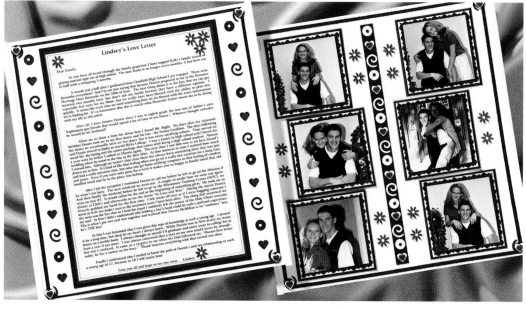

Lindsey's Love Letter

PUNCH SIMPLE SHAPES TO "SET OFF" NEWS TO FAMILY

Cut ⅜" black paper borders; mount. Punch and layer small black spiral, small white heart and mini red heart; mount. Outline printed journaling in red ink; double mat. Quadruple mat photos; trimming with decorative scissors. Mount a ½ x 11" black strip between the photos. Punch small circles, hearts, spirals and daisies; layer with mini hearts and ⅛" circles.

Laurie Nelson Capener, Providence, Utah

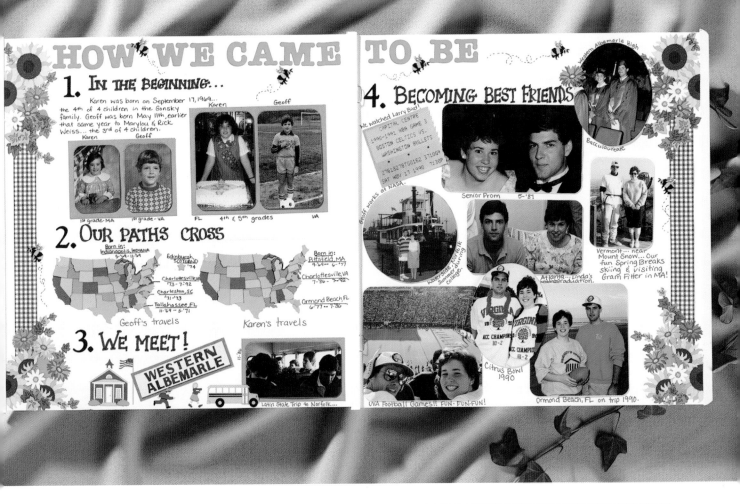

How We Came To Be

ILLUSTRATE THE JOURNEY FROM BIRTH TO "I DO"

(ABOVE) Mount ¾" gingham strips on left and right layout edges. Layer flower and vine stickers (Mrs. Grossman's) in each corner. Adhere letter and number stickers (Creative Memories) for page titles. Layer photos and memorabilia with additional themed stickers.

(RIGHT) Cut ½" red strips into brick shapes and mount as shown along left border. Freehand cut gemstone for die cut ring (Accu-Cut); adhere. Layer photos and adhere pink word stickers (Creative Memories).

Karen Weiss, Edmond, Oklahoma

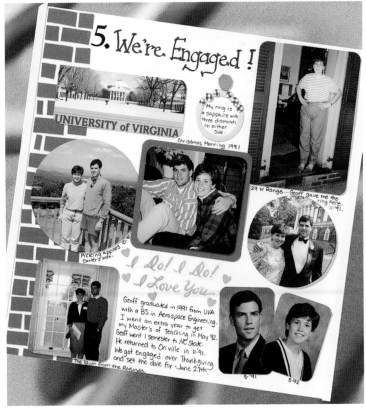

N ikki chose to limit her album theme to subtle colors for a simple, sentimental look.

The well-planned use of light-colored inks, hand-drawn lettering and flower stamps (Close To My Heart/D.O.T.S.) creates a soft mood for her pages.

Her use of engagement clippings and photos are a great "lead in" to the rest of the wedding album.

Our Engagement Photos...

Nikki Raye Snodgrass
Fiancee of David Byron Probert
Snodgrass and Probert planning July wedding

The engagement of Nikki Raye Snodgrass to David Byron Probert has been announced by their parents.

Miss Snodgrass is the daughter of Susan and Bob Bruffett, Jasper, and Larry Snodgrass, Golden City. Maternal grandmother is Mrs. Goldie Yoke, Liberal. Paternal grandparents are Mr. and Mrs. Vernon Snodgrass, Liberal.

She is a 1987 graduate of Jasper High School and is attending Mis-souri Southern State College part-time. She is employed at Finley Engineering Co., Lamar.

The prospective bridegroom is the son of Kenneth and Judy Probert, Golden City. Maternal grand-mother is Mrs. J.L. Morton, Golden City.

He is a 1983 graduate of Golden City High School and is employed at Cardinal Scale Manufacturing, Webb City.

A July 20 wedding is planned.

Snodgrass-Probert

The engagement of Nikki Raye Snod-grass to David Byron Probert has been announced. She is the daughter of Susan and Bob Bruffett, Jasper, and Lar-ry Snodgrass, Golden City. He is the son of Kenneth and Ju-dy Probert, Golden City.

The bride-to-be is a 1987 grad-uate of Jasper High School and is attending Mis-souri Southern State College. She is employed by Finley Engineering Co., Lamar.

A 1983 graduate of Golden City High School, the prospective bridegroom is employed by Cardinal Scale Manufactur-ing Co., Webb City.

A July 20 wedding is being planned.

Nikki Snodgrass

David Byron Probert proposed marriage to Nikki Raye Snodgrass on February 9, 1991.

They chose an engagement ring and David put it on her finger on Valentine's Day, February 14, 1991.

Church Shower

This wonderful bridal shower was held at the United Methodist Church in Golden City, MO. It was hosted by Ona Thomas, Lila West and Melita Jackson at 2:00 on June 15, 1991. We received many gifts, including a beautiful lavender and white quilt handmade by my Grandmother Viola Snodgrass. It was very nice.

The Gift Table

Grandma's Quilt!

Melita

Melita, Lila, Ona and Nikki

Gudry Probert

The Hostesses

Michelle Ehrsam

Susan Bruffett

Michelle

"Don't break the ribbons!"

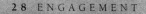

By allowing journaling to help her photos tell the story, Nikki captured the spirit behind a new tradition...

Stitched with Love

My wedding dress is very special to me because my future mother-in-law, Judy Probert and I made it. We worked on it primarily in the evenings. I would try it on from time to time to model it for Doug's Grandmother Aileen Morton. She wasn't able to help us but She enjoyed watching our progress.

All the buttons in the back.

Judy takes a closer look.

Julee Probert helps me with my shoes.

HERE COMES THE BRIDE

Before Eric presented me to my husband-to-be, I paused momentarily at my mother, Susan Bruffett's aisle and gave her a hug, kiss and a flower from my bouquet. On our way out of the church after the ceremony, we paused and did the same for my new mother-in-law, Judy Probert.

Nikki Raye Snodgrass was walked down the aisle and was given in marriage by her brother, Eric Jeffrey Snodgrass on July 20, 1991. He looked so serious and handsome in his tuxedo.

You May Kiss The Bride...

The Kiss...

...pausing before the ceremony to give her mother a hug, a kiss and a flower from her bouquet and pausing after the ceremony to do the same for her new mother-in-law.

Lynleigh Heslep & Chad Fast

Mr. & Mrs. David B. Probert

Please join us for a
Champagne Bridal Shower
honoring
Julie Cullinane
Sunday, July 19, 1998
12:30 p.m.
Monarch Bay Club
Laguna Niguel

Kindly respond to
Nanci Aguilar
800-722-2367
ext. 2171

Bridal Shower

BLESSED IS THE

BRIDE-TO-BE,

SHOWERED WITH GIFTS

OF GENEROSITY.

For centuries, friends and family have shown their love and support of a bride by hosting a bridal shower. Traditionally intended to help a bride "set up housekeeping" with practical things, today's showers lend themselves to imaginative gift-giving, from kitchen gadgets and recipes to linens and lingerie and more.

In your scrapbook, try to include photos of guests, whether in a group or individually with the bride-to-be. Photos of the gifts, cake, refreshments, decorations, shower activities and the actual invitation provide for memorable pages.

JULIE'S CHAMPAGNE BRIDAL SHOWER
YUKO NEAL
HUNTINGTON BEACH, CALIFORNIA
(SEE PAGE 124)

Bridal Showers

For page backgrounds, trim sheets of gray paper with decorative scissors. Use thin black pen to draw title letters and hearts on pink paper. Cut out title words and round corners. Use white opaque pen to outline title words. Draw additional white lines inside each letter. Silhouette cut extra photos and layer in a group. Adhere umbrella and gift stickers (Creative Memories).

Jenny Hollibaugh, Lincoln, Nebraska

Bridesmaid Luncheon

VELLUM AND BORDER JOURNALING ADD ELEGANCE

Mount sheet of printed vellum paper (The Paper Co.) on sage background. Mat photos and arrange with invitation. Add ribbon (Offray) bow. Journal with white opaque pen. Adhere daisy sticker (Frances Meyer).

Donna Pittard, Kingwood, Texas

Showers of Love
of Love

April 17

Showers of Love
STAMP A SWIRLING WATER THEME

Draw line border on bottom page background first and stamp hearts (Stampin' Up!) as explained below. Mat 1⅞ x 11" rectangle and 8½" square of striped paper (Royal Stationery) with white. Trim mats with jumbo scallop scissors and punch ⅛" holes for lace effect. Mount square and rectangle. Stamp swirls (Stampin' Up!) as shown. Stamp, heat emboss and cut out watering can (Stampin' Up!). Punch small red hearts. Cut stencil letters (Pebbles In My Pocket) for title. Mat photos and arrange. Journal and draw line borders with thin pen.

Joyce Schweitzer
Greensboro, North Carolina

STAMPING A BACKGROUND

Stamping background designs are an easy way to decorate a scrapbook. To stamp the heart background shown at right, first cover the page edges with removable tape. Then randomly stamp the design in the exposed areas. You can vary the look of a stamped background by overlapping stamped designs, combining several stamps or ink colors, heat embossing or stamping several times before re-inking. For a tone-on-tone look, choose an ink color slightly darker than the background. (See page 75 for basic stamping tips.)

Liz's Round-the-Clock Shower

Betsy and her mother-in-law wanted to have a unique shower for their friend, Liz. They settled on a Round-the-Clock Shower. When guests called to RSVP, they were able to pick a time of day their gift would represent and the gifts were opened in the chronological order of the clock.

"Many of the guests already had a gift in mind, so it was easy for them to pick a time of day to match that gift. For others, it was a fun challenge to find gifts for certain times of day. It was great to see what people came up with," says Betsy.

Liz's well-timed gifts included an 8:00 a.m. toaster to use before her mad dash to the office; 9:00 a.m. pancake mix, syrup and bowl in case there was no mad dash to the office; 2:00 p.m. fully loaded picnic basket; 5:00 p.m. hors d'oeuvres platter from Mexico; 5:30 p.m. pedicure kit for those tired feet; 11:00 p.m. flashlight to get to the bathroom safely and a water decanter set to combat midnight thirst.

Liz loved the unique shower and enjoyed her timely gifts.

Betsy Cruickshank, Portland, Oregon

TRADITIONAL ROLES OF MAID/MATRON OF HONOR AND BRIDESMAIDS

- *Assist bride in wedding planning*
- *Assist bride in addressing invitations, assembling favors, decorating, etc.*
- *Attend fittings*
- *Help at or host showers*
- *Attend wedding rehearsal*
- *Attend photo shoots*
- *Arrange bridal train and veil at ceremony*
- *Hold bride's bouquet during ceremony*
- *Hold groom's ring until needed during ceremony*
- *Official wedding witness who signs marriage license*

Bridal Shower Keepsake Cookbook

CREATE A TREASURED GIFT OF GUESTS' RECIPES FOR THE BRIDE-TO-BE

Ask each bridal shower guest to bring a favorite recipe. At the shower, have each guest
transfer their recipe to a recipe card and decorate the card using basic scrapbooking supplies.
Photograph each guest with the bride-to-be as well as the guests busy creating their cards.
Later, assemble all recipes and photos into a keepsake cookbook album for the bride-to-be.

Leemay Hritz, Van Nuys, California

Announcement Tea
September 29, 1991

Tea
honoring
Donna Elizabeth Waldrip
bride elect of
Scott Thomas Pittard
Sunday, September 29, 1991
two until four
643 Camark Ave.
Camden, Arkansas

Mrs. Edwin M. Horton
Mrs. Lil Andrisos
Mrs. Cecil Counce
Mrs. Robert Fisher

Mrs. W. A. Graves, Jr.
Mrs. W. J. Lester, Jr.
Mrs. Terry Merritt
Mrs. Charles Plunkett

Leslie, Donna & Cindy

Shirley & Donna open a gift from the Hostess

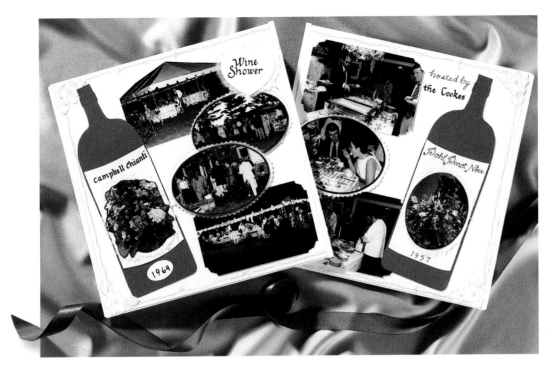

UNIQUE BRIDAL SHOWERS

ABC *Gifts relate to letters of the alphabet.*
ADVENTURE *Weekend retreat at spa or resort.*
BASKET *Baskets filled with gifts for certain rooms.*
BON VOYAGE *Travel-related gifts.*
BRIDE'S NAME *Gifts begin with letter from bride's name.*
BY-MAIL *Out-of-state relatives and college friends participate in gift-giving by mail; opening of gifts is videotaped and mailed to "guests."*
FAMILY TREASURES *Heirlooms and heirloom-quality gifts.*
GOURMET *For the discriminating cook or connoisseur.*
GREEN *Earth-friendly gifts.*
HOLIDAY OR CALENDAR *Gifts are holiday decorations.*
HOME IMPROVEMENT *Gifts of tools and 'guy stuff.'*
JACK & JILL COED *Barbeque or cocktail party for couples.*
LINEN *Towels, sheets, soaps, etc. in bride's colors.*
LINGERIE *Especially for the bride who has everything.*
PET *Gifts for the couple's esteemed pets.*
RECIPE *Kitchen gifts along with recipes to cook and recipes for the soul.*
ROUND-THE-CLOCK *Gifts correlate with a time of day.*
SCRAPBOOK *Gifts related to scrapbooking and recording family history.*
WINE-TASTING *Often at a local vineyard; gifts of wine from couple's birth years.*

Wine Shower

CREATE BOTTLE LABELS WITH NAMES AND BIRTH YEARS

(ABOVE) Use silver and gold pens to draw wavy lines and embellishments along layout edges. For each corner, layer two birch leaves and one large flower punched from handmade paper (The Paper Co.). Draw flower and leaf details with silver pen. Hand-cut wine bottles and labels. Label wines using bride's and groom's last names and birth years. Snip corners of rectangular photos with decorative scissors. Double mat oval and silhouetted photos with black and handmade paper. Mat heart for title with hand-made paper. Tear hand-made paper mats for a feathery effect, or trim mats using decorative scissors.

Sandra Yanisko, Barto, Pennsylvania

Announcement Tea

SUMMARIZE SHOWER WITH BEST PHOTOS

(LEFT) Mount ¼" forest green strips on edges of terra cotta background. Journal on border and write title with bronze pen. Mat photos with forest green paper and title and invitation with handmade paper. Mount die-cut frame (Gina Bear) over invitation. Layer leaf stickers (Francis Meyer) around photos. Caption photos with gold pen.

Donna Pittard, Kingwood, Texas

ABC wedding albums are a fun alternative to the "chronological order" album. Each page or layout features photos, memorabilia and design elements that relate to a certain letter of the alphabet.

Kelly's pages successfully document cherished wedding elements through the use of actual memorabilia, cropped photos and journaling.

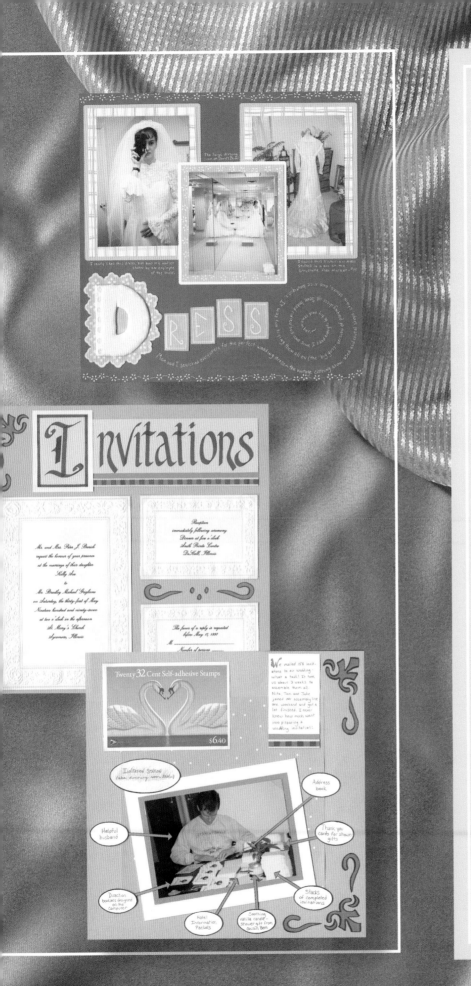

ABC WORD LIST

A accessories, adorned, aisle, altar, announcement, antique, arch, attendants
B bachelor, bachelorette, bagpipes, balloon, band, bells, best man, Bible, blue, borrowed, bouquet, boutonniere, bow, bridal, bride, bridesmaids, bride-to-be, butterflies
C candles, candle-lighting, cake, camera, candid, caterer, celebration, ceremony, champagne, cherish, church, colors, confetti, corsage, countdown, couple, courtship
D dad, dainty, dance, dating, daughter, dazzling, decorations, diamond, dinner, doily, dove, dress, drink
E early, earring, eat, elegant, embroidered, encourage, engagement, engraved, enjoy, entertainment, exhausted, exit, exiting
F fairy tale, faith, family, father, favors, favorite, feather, first, flowers, flower girl, food, forever, formal, friends, fun, future
G garden, garland, garter, getaway, gift, gloves, God, gold, gown, gracious, grandparent, grin, groom, groomsmen, groom's cake, guest book, guests
H hair, hand-stitched, handkerchief, happily ever after, happiness, headpiece, health, heart, heirloom, heritage, honeymoon, hope, hors d'oeuvres, hotel, hour, husband
I icing, imagine, incredible, invitations, inspiration, instruments, irresistible
J jewelry, journal, joy, jump, just married
K keepsake, kids, kiss, knot
L lace, lady, lake, lasting, laughter, legacy, limousine, lingerie, location, love
M magic, magnificent, maid of honor, make-up, marriage, marriage license, matrimony, matron of honor, meal, memories, menu, minister, mom, money, mother, music
N name, napkin, necklace, nephew, new, news, newspaper, niece, nightgown
O ocean, official, officiant, old, organist, out-of-town
P parents, party, pearls, petals, photograph, pillow, poem, portraits, prayer, prepare, present, processional
Q quality, queasy, question, quick, quilt
R ready, receipts, reception, registry, rehearsal, relax, remember, reunion, ribbon, ring bearer, rings, rite, ritual, romantic, rose
S satin, shimmering, shower, silk, silver, six-pence, sleep, son, special, star, sun, surprise
T table, taffeta, tea, tent, threshold, time, tired, toast, together, tradition, train, travel, treasure, trumpet, tulle, tuxedo
U umbrella, unbelievable, under, underwater, unforgettable, unique
V vacation, valuable, veil, very, vibrant, vineyard, violin, vivid, voice, vows
W weather, wed, wedding, welcome, whisper, white, wife, wise, wish, wonderful
X x-cellent, x-pert, x-tra, x-traordinary
Y yes, young, youthful, yummy
Z zany, zestful, zzzzzzzz...

Denise's Bachelorette Party July 11, 1997

the Bride-to-be

Denise & Cory are huge Rockies fans so... Nikki & Lisa planed her bachelorette party to start at Coors Field for a game

Denise and auntie

DENVER

DATES/TIMES SUBJECT TO CHANGE. SEE CONDITIONS ON BACK
FRI JUL 11 1997 7:05 PM
NO REFUNDS OR EXCHANGES
COORS FIELD
SAN DIEGO PADRES
vs
COLORADO ROCKIES

Laura & Toni Vescio

Take me out to t...
tak...

Bachelor and Bachelorette Parties

CELEBRATE WITH FRIENDS

THIS SEASON OF CHANGE

AND THE JOY OF

A NEW BEGINNING.

This once all-male revelry dates back to 5th-century Sparta, where soldiers feasted and toasted one another on a wedding's eve. It's a time for nervous grooms and jittery brides to spend a fun-filled evening with their wedding party and close friends to celebrate the end of being single and the new journey into matrimony.

Whether your party was at a comedy club, a hotel suite, or just a night on the town, be sure to preserve this evening in pictures. Your photos and memorabilia are sure to capture enough mischief, pranks and horseplay to last a lifetime.

DENISE'S BACHELORETTE PARTY
EILEEN RUSCETTA
WESTMINSTER, COLORADO
(SEE PAGE 124)

Lisa's Scavenger Hunt Bachelorette Party

On a January night in 1998, Nikki hosted a zany, fun-filled bachelorette party for her sister, Lisa. The scavenger hunt party was held at the Christie Lodge in Vail, Colorado. Lisa knew about the bachelorette party, but the scavenger hunt was a complete surprise. Nikki had fashioned scavenger hunt instructional medallions to a costume necklace and presented it to Lisa.

With a mock bridal veil perched on her head, medallions around her neck and school and college chums (even her college sorority mom) in tow, Lisa set out for a night on the town to follow some outright hysterical instructions.

She had to retrieve pocket lint from a stranger's pocket, have a man perform a "Here Comes the Bride" serenade for her, talk a lounge owner into buying her a cocktail and, among other comedic tasks, have her photo taken with a police officer who jovially handcuffed her as well.

Lisa was a great sport and everyone was in stitches with laughter. They capped off the evening with dinner and a big pajama party, complete with gifts of lingerie.

Eileen Ruscetta, Westminster, Colorado

Kristen's Secrets

KRISTEN'S SECRETS ARE REVEALED

Mount pink hearts and pink striped paper (Paper Patch) to hot pink background. Adhere ¼" gold paper strip atop seam where printed papers meet. Double-mat photos with pink and hot pink paper. Attach hand-cut, stamped (Stampin' Up!) and embossed (see page 74 for embossing technique) hearts and sticker letters (Frances Meyer).

Joyce Schweitzer, Greensboro, North Carolina

TRADITIONAL ROLES OF BEST MAN AND GROOMSMEN

- Attend or host parties or showers
- Attend fitting and rent appropriate attire
- Attend wedding rehearsal
- Bring marriage license to ceremony
- Attend photo shoots
- Hold bride's ring until needed in ceremony
- Official wedding witness who signs marriage license
- Serve as ushers before and after ceremony
- Deliver payment to officiant, musicians, other vendors
- Propose first toast during reception
- Return all formal wear

Adrenalin Adventures

SHOWCASE BACHELOR PARTY IN THE SKY

Adhere trimmed, hand-stenciled cloud template (All Night Media) paper to blue checkered paper (MPR Assoc.) background. Mount photos on red paper. Adhere flying ducks photocopied from coloring book (Suzy's Zoo) and journal.

Joyce Schweitzer, Greensboro, North Carolina

Kimberly Herbert to Paul Householder

MARRIED AUGUST 13, 1994   UPPER MARLBORO, MARYLAND

Once upon a time...

Patrice Hagmann of Montclair, Virginia, created this very special "fairy tale" album as a memento of her brother Paul's wedding. Her extensive journaling captures the romance of the wedding ceremony. Delicate pink and green scroll work adds enchantment while pulling together the album's pages in perfect harmony.

Dearly Beloved,

We are gathered here today, in the sight of God, and in the presence of these witnesses to join together Kim and Paul in holy matrimony, which is an honorable estate, signifying to us the mystical union between Christ and His church....

...which holy estate Christ adorned and beautified in Cana of Galilee. It is not to be entered into unadvisedly, but reverently, discreetly, and in the fear of God.

I remind you both, as you stand in the presence of God, to remember that love and loyalty alone will avail as the foundation of a happy and enduring home. If the solemn vows you are about to make are kept faithfully, and if steadfastly you endeavor to do the will of God, your lives will be full of joy, and the home you are establishing will abide in peace. No other ties are more tender, no other vows more sacred than those you now assume.

Who presents this woman to be married to this man?

Her mother and I.

No fairy tale album would be complete without a "Once upon a time..." title page (shown above) and a "They lived happily ever after..." closing page.

Our Vows

I, Paul, take you Kim, to be my wedded wife, to have and to hold, from this day forward, for better, for worse, for richer, for poorer, in sickness and in health, to love and to cherish, till death us do part, according to God's holy ordinance, and thereto I pledge you my faith.

A man and woman stand before us with eyes and hearts only for each other. Somewhere and sometime in their recent history they saw each other. That eternal click of emotion and attention, and a feeling that would grow and mature into a love that now here is embraced and declared till death they do part.

I, Kim, take you Paul, to be my wedded husband, to have and to hold, from this day forward, for better, for worse, for richer, for poorer, in sickness and in health, to love and to cherish, till death us do part, according to God's holy ordinance, and thereto I pledge you my faith.

Eternal God, creator and preserver of us all, give to all spiritual grace, send your blessing upon Kim and Paul, whom we bless in your name, that they may surely perform and keep the covenant made this day. May they ever remain in perfect love and peace together, and live according to your holy laws. Look graciously upon them, that they may honor and cherish each other and live in faithfulness and patience, in wisdom and true godliness that their home may be a haven of blessing and peace.

Using your own photos and words, your family and friends become the cast of characters and your wedding location becomes an enchanted land in a fairy tale wedding album.

The Toast

We listen as Josh does the honors, wishing us well, thanking Paul for his friendship over the years, and shocking the older folks with an irreverent reference to our wedding night.

Even Justin and Kevin raise a glass to the happiness of the couple!

To our future!

Contemporary Weddings

WHEN I FALL IN LOVE,

IT WILL BE FOREVER.

WHEN I GIVE MY

HEART, IT WILL BE

COMPLETELY.

-Edward Heyman

CHAD AND FAITH WALLIS
LORNA DEE CHRISTENSEN
CORVALLIS, OREGON
(SEE PAGE 124)

Your wedding was a carefully choreographed event to orchestrate. You followed your heart and it led to today. A day filled with promise and hope, magic and the awe-inspiring mystery of love itself.

Whether your wedding was simple and serene, profound and passionate, textbook traditional or contemporary, it was your day of memories that you will want to relive over and over again.

In the pages that follow, see how some brides have preserved their guests' signatures in special ways. And how others have created pages for

CONTINUED. . .

dress rehearsals, wedding preparation, walking down the aisle, ceremony highlights and those all-important formal portraits. Learn a new technique to add to your wedding pages or, perhaps, create a one-of-a-kind miniature album using your wedding photos.

With so many momentous photos and treasured keepsakes to remember the day by, you are guaranteed some beautiful scrapbook pages that promptly whisk you back to your day of "I do."

Kristen and Chadwick's Title Page
ILLUMINATE PRINTED PAPERS IN GOLD

(UPPER RIGHT) Mount printed paper (Frances Meyer) to page. Emphasize window detail by embossing with clear embossing pen (EK Success) and add gold detail embossing powder. See page 74 for more on embossing technique.

Joyce Schweitzer
Greensboro, North Carolina

LEEMAY HRITZ
VAN NUYS, CALIFORNIA
(SEE PAGE 124)

Deborah and Chris Photograph Their Own Wedding

Deborah, a wedding photographer, met her future husband in the camera store where she rented her camera equipment and he worked. When Deborah and Chris eloped to Jamaica in 1995, it seemed only natural to the newlyweds to photograph the wedding themselves.

They used a tripod and a remote control device that clicked the shutter every ten seconds during the ceremony. Then they posed for the shots of the two of them together.

"We took each other's portraits for the remainder of the photos," says Deborah. "Although it did feel as though we were working on our wedding day, in the end we were glad we had made the effort to capture the memories of our special day."

Deborah Handley and Chris Williams
Annapolis, Maryland

The card reads:

Kristen Leigh Williams
and
Chadwick Wayne Pruett
were united in
Holy Matrimony
on the 5th day of June 1999
at Grace Moravian Church

This is my Beloved,
This is my Friend.
Song of Solomon 5:16

Michael and Melinda
1997
A Love Story
from A - Z

Michael and Melinda's Title Page

BUILD A PUNCH ART WREATH

Weave ½" wide strips of white paper over entire page to create lattice and adhere. Punch large blue flowers, large green birch leaves and medium hearts; assemble punched shapes into circle wreath, cutting some birch leaves in half. Add white hearts for buds. Attach vine die cuts (Accu-Cut). Accent with punched flowers and leaves. Embellish flowers and leaves with white pen.

Deiga Brummett, San Bernardino, California

Guests' Signatures Photo Mat

YOUR GUESTS CREATE AN ALTERNATIVE TO THE TRADITIONAL WEDDING GUEST BOOK

Have a 12 x 12" photo mat cut to accommodate a 4 x 6" or 5 x 7" photo.
Before taking it to your wedding ceremony, apply removable artist's tape around the mat's outer edge and where
you may wish to place a nameplate. The tape will serve as a "place holder" to prevent guests' signatures from
being covered later by the frame or journaling. Set out smudge-proof pigment pens or markers of choice
for guests to use. After the wedding, frame a favorite wedding photo, vows or a small copy of your
marriage certificate in the window; frame with a 12 x 12" frame (Puzzlemates).

Guest Book Pages

MOUNT GUEST BOOK PAGES INTO SCRAPBOOK ALBUM

Why keep a book in storage when there's only been a few pages used? One simple solution is to carefully remove the pages of guests' signatures from the guest book and mount on pages of your choice in your wedding scrapbook; stamp rosebud and vine border (Close To My Heart/D.O.T.S.).

Alana Zeller, Simi Valley, California

Guest Book Flip Pages

CREATE FLIP PAGES USING GUESTS' WELL-WISHES

Supply 4 x 4" squares of printed paper of choice for guests to record their well-wishes, memories and comments. Use printed background paper of choice; layer and mount squares in flip-style as shown, mounting bottom pages first and working upward. Accent as desired.

Caroline LeBel, Toronto, Ontario, Canada

Mini Guest Book Pages

REDUCE COPIES OF GUEST BOOK PAGES TO FIT INTO ALBUM

Scan actual guest signature pages; edit pages to 2 x 2½" in size. Print in color. Or color photocopy guest signature pages, reducing until pages are 2 x 2½" in size. Mount mini copies on colored paper trimmed with fancy scissors; adhere around photos of guest book attendant and guests.

Stephanie Hofmeister, Coronado, California

Some of the most laughable, endearing and unforgettable events happen in those fleeting moments before the ceremony. Keep plenty of film on hand to seize these unpredictable moments.

Dress Rehearsal

QUILT A DIAMOND AND HEXAGON DESIGN

(LEFT) Use geometric template to cut six hexagon and six diamond photos. Cut an additional hexagon for the title. Mat hexagons and trim with decorative scissors. Arrange pieces on light green paper and trim edges with decorative scissors. Mount quilt design on forest green background. Write title and draw stitch lines with white opaque and gold pens.

Cyndi Malefyt, Grand Rapids, Michigan

My Wedding Handkerchief

DOCUMENT A CHERISHED WEDDING TRADITION

(LOWER FAR RIGHT) Cut two 2" navy squares and two 1½" gingham squares in half diagonally. Layer triangles in page corners. Use wavy ruler to trim edges of printed poem. Mat poem with navy paper. Punch mat corners with corner rounder and hearts corner decoration punch. Triple mat oval photo. Tie sheer ribbon bow and arrange around poem. Trim printed journaling with decorative scissors.

Eileen Ruscetta, Westminster, Colorado

Let's Toast

EMBOSS OVERLAPPING HEARTS

(LOWER RIGHT) Use purple paper for page background. Stamp and heat emboss lavender and purple hearts (Stampin' Up!) on left edge of 11" striped square (Keeping Memories Alive). Trim left edge along heart outlines. Cut slits along right edges of bottom three hearts. Slip left edge of rectangular photo beneath cut-out areas. Mat oval photos and trim with decorative scissors. Use letter (Making Memories) and small heart (Mrs. Grossman's) stickers for title.

Joyce Schweitzer, Greensboro, North Carolina

Rehearsal Dinner

MAKE A TABLE SETTING
OF GUEST PHOTOS

Mount a rectangular photo in
the page center. Cut six photos
into 4" circles for "plates."
Fold 1" gingham squares in
half diagonally for napkins.
Adhere fork, knife and spoon
stickers (Mrs. Grossman's) to
complete each place setting.
Journal with thick silver pen.

Eileen Ruscetta
Westminster, Colorado

A mother is a mother still,
the holiest thing alive.

A last minute check on my veil.

A Mother Is a Mother Still

MAT A FAVORITE PORTRAIT

Trim photo mats with decorative scissors.
Write title with thick black pen. Draw dots on
inner mat and write caption with thin black pen.

Jane Johnson, Danville, California

Marriage Suits Us

MAKE A "FITTING" PENGUIN SUIT PAGE

Mount white sheet of paper diagonally on black
background and trim corners. Mat photos with
white and black gingham (Paper Patch) paper.
Print and mat title. Adhere penguin stickers
(Mrs. Grossman's).

Jody Weber, Lafayette, Indiana

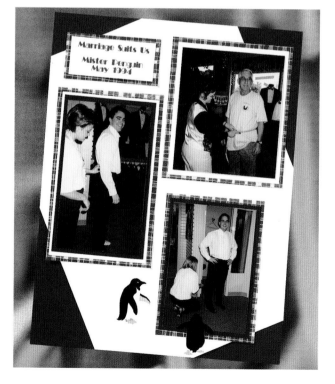

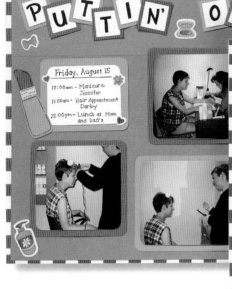

Puttin' on the Ritz

HAVE FUN WITH WEDDING DAY DRESS-UP

Mount strips of pink checkerboard paper (Paper Patch) on page edges. Center an 11" purple square on each page. Mat 1" white squares with aqua and pink paper and write title letters with thick black pen. Freehand cut pieces for lipstick and nail polish. Adhere cosmetics, flower and heart stickers (Frances Meyer).

Carrie Davis, Everett, Washington

Getting Ready

ACCENT WITH PRINTED FLORAL PAPER

Mat photos, title and journaling with plum paper. Mat once or twice again with floral printed paper (Keeping Memories Alive). Cut additional flowers from paper for corner embellishments.

Jenny Hollibaugh, Lincoln, Nebraska

THE CEREMONY

Every ritual of your ceremony holds special meaning, from the ceremony location to the custom vows. By weaving into your scrapbook the stories behind your vows, the candle-lighting or traditions performed at the ceremony, you can reproduce your ceremony's setting and mood for all generations to understand.

Here Comes The Bride!

CREATE A CHURCH AISLE

Use printed paper (Sunrise Publications) for background. Double mat single photo at left with navy paper and printed paper (Keeping Memories Alive); adhere. Hand-cut mat for "aisle" photo from printed paper and include "runner" that extends to bottom of page. Add brown paper and vellum to runner; accent with stickers and punched mini flowers. Adhere candle and corner stickers (NRN Designs) as shown. Add letter stickers (Frances Meyer) and other stickers (Creative Memories) to complete design.

Linda Gibbs
Kennewick, Washington

For one special day, flowers enhance many dreams. And like weddings, flowers are short-lived. That's why it's only natural to want to preserve your flowers and greenery from bouquets and centerpieces in your wedding scrapbook pages.

PRESSING FLOWERS

Pressing flowers is easy. The old-fashioned "heavy book and absorbent paper" pressing method is still a favorite method. Carefully arrange dry, fresh flowers and petals on a flat sheet of paper towel or facial tissue making certain none of the flowers are touching. Cover the arrangement with another piece of absorbent paper and add weight on top. Check for neatly pressed flowers in three days to six weeks, depending on flower size.

STORING FLOWERS

Pressed flowers can be stored in glassine sleeves until ready to mount. Use tweezers and acid-free, photo-safe liquid or tape adhesives to mount flowers to scrapbook pages. If protected from light and moisture, your pressed flowers should last indefinitely. Because flowers are organic, the potential for acidic interaction with your photographs is high. Treat pressed flowers as memorabilia and don't let them directly touch your photos. Be sure to use page protectors or encapsulate the pressed flowers in self-adhesive memorabilia pockets. Although the color intensity may fade over time, your pressed flowers will retain a timeless, nostalgic beauty that adds to the rich visual record of your wedding.

Lisa and Douglas

FLOWER STICKERS, A CONVENIENT ALTERNATIVE

Hand-cut purchased card. Insert photo and journaling; mount on page. Adhere pressed flower stickers (Pressed Petals) as shown. Attach pressed ribbon bow. Draw flower fronds with gold pen.

Pat Murray, Edmonton, Alberta, Canada

BEST FLOWERS FOR PRESSING

Flowers with low moisture content and thin petals work best. Some flower varieties that work well for pressing are alyssum, coreopsis, coral bells, cosmos, daisy, fern, fuchsia, forget-me-not, ivy, larkspur, lobelia, Queen Ann's lace, and verbena. Thicker flowers, like roses, carnations and mums, press best when they are thinned or if their petals are separated and pressed individually.

Mrs. Terri Pruett Moser, Soloist

Mrs. Kathy Pruett, Organist

Nancy and Kevin Lewand

HERE COMES THE BRIDE

Organist and Soloist

SHOW THOSE WHO PLAYED A PART

(UPPER FAR LEFT) Use printed paper (NRN Designs) for page background. Triple mat photos with lavender, gold and mauve paper. Draw line borders around inner and outer mats.

Joyce Schweitzer, Greensboro, North Carolina

Nancy and Kevin

BUILD A VINE-COVERED CANOPY

(UPPER LEFT) Mount ¼" white strips around left, top and right sides of photo to form canopy structure. Punch leaves and flowers using small maple leaf punch and tulip trimmed from small tulip punch. Punch small white butterflies and draw dashed lines. Accent title with additional punched shapes.

Nancy Johns, Chicago, Illinois

Here Comes the Bride

RECORD THE WEDDING MARCH

(LOWER LEFT) Mount 8½ x 11" sheet of emerald green paper in page center. Mat oval photos with cream paper. Trim mats with decorative scissors. Slice and separate photos for right page. Adhere letters (Creative Memories), gold silhouette stickers (Mark Ent.) and white flower (Mrs. Grossman's) stickers. Draw details around flower stickers.

Pam Friis, Castle Rock, Colorado

I Now Pronounce You Husband and Wife

CRAFT A LAYERED PHOTO AND PAPER WEDDING CROSS

(ABOVE) Cut cross outline from printed paper (Frances Meyer) and save scraps. Cut points from 5½" gold sparkle sticker circle (Sandylion) to form center star, also saving scraps. Trim decorative corners of center square photo and save scraps. Draw a pencil guideline for journaling using a 6" circle template. Layer scraps for corner decorations.

Mary Lisenby, Wichita, Kansas

Stained Glass Extravaganza

REPRODUCE STAINED GLASS WINDOWS

Mount black paper on a double page spread. Assemble hand-cut pieces of colored paper "shards" in patterns that mimic stained glass window in photos. Overlay photos, cropping as necessary to fit. Adhere photos and colored paper bits.

Jo-Ann Richardson Sickles, Everett, Washington

The Two Shall Become One

MAKE A FOLD-OUT CARD TO ACCOMMODATE JOURNALING

Add more space to scrapbook pages by creating a fold-out card for text-heavy pages.
Continue design or embellishments of the scrapbook page onto the fold-out for a unified look.

Yvonne Laura Torres, Miami, Florida

VOWS SWEETLY SPOKEN, MAY THEY NEVER BE BROKEN

Many couples add the ultimate personal touch to the wedding ceremony by writing part or all of their own vows. If you wish to write your own vows, consider these tips:

- *Include things that are unique and special to you*
- *Talk about the moment you fell in love*
- *Tell how your mate has changed or added to your life*
- *Add personal promises made to each other*
- *Weave in a special prayer or blessing*
- *Highlight an inspirational marriage reading*

- *Showcase a favorite love poem*
- *Use words from beloved songs*
- *Visit the library for books on wedding readings*
- *Avoid private, highly personal issues*
- *Avoid inside jokes*

Coin Book Miniature Photo Keepsake

PRESERVING WEDDING PHOTOS IN AN HISTORIC FASHION

During the 1960s an English coin collector noticed an odd little crack around the outer edge of an old European commemorative coin dating back to 1639. He poked around at the crack and out popped a tiny round book with seventeen tiny round pages connected by ribbon. Each "page" contained a miniature painting or scene from the life of Protestant Reformation leader, Martin Luther, 1483-1546.

Our contemporary version of this unique little album preserves wedding photos in a similar manner and is destined to become an heirloom treasure.

1. Crop 14 1⅞" photos using a circle cutter (Lion Office Products). Crop 14 pieces of colored paper the same size for photo backing. Pre-arrange photos in diamond pattern as shown, selecting one photo for the 2" round tin (Lee Valley Tools, Ltd.) and one to be the last one adhered to ribbon bottom. Cover tin's glass and paint tin gold.

2. Adhere 14" length of 1" wide ribbon to bottom of tin; mount photo atop ribbon in tin. Glue one 9½" and two 5½" ribbon "crossbars" to vertical ribbon, leaving 1½" between each ribbon. Mount photos and backing on ribbons at ½" intervals to create the diamond pattern shown. Journal on paper backing, if desired.

3. To fold photos back into tin, begin folding all photos on crossbar ribbons in toward vertical ribbon. Then start at bottom photo as shown, folding all photos upward until you reach the tin. Place photos in tin with bottom photo showing through glass lid. Accent lid with couple's initials (Mark Ent.), if desired.

Christine Bechert to Nicholas MacIlvaine

MARRIED JULY 19, 1998 RINGWOOD, NEW JERSEY

There are no rules and regulations in contemporary wedding ceremonies, and Christine and Nick's self-styled ceremony was no exception. Christine silhouetted some photos but the majority are standard photos whose corners have been slipped into mat slots created with a slot punch (Family Treasures). The consistent photo treatments and the double-matted journaling gives the album its clean, museum-like quality.

She's so beautiful, she looks like his mother.

My brother DID A SUPER JOB CHOOSING ALL OUR WINE FOR OUR WEDDING AND REHEARSAL PARTY. HE EVEN MADE UP WINE LISTS AND SERVED AS PARTENDER DURING THE WEDDING. HIS RECENT TRIP TO ITALY HELPED HIM PICK FABULOUS WINES—EVERYONE LOVED THEM! HE ALSO SENT NICK AND I OUR FAVORITE WINE FROM OUR REHEARSAL PARTY FOR OUR FIRST WEDDING ANNIVERSARY. NICK AND I SHARED THE BOTTLE TOGETHER WHILE EATING OUR DEFROSTED CAKE & WATCHING OUR WEDDING VIDEO. WHAT A GREAT BROTHER! (WINE CIRO 1990)

our Wedding *july 19, 1998*

Circle of Love

"WITH THIS RING

I THEE WED..."

Two hearts...
one life...
one love.

Wedding Vows

I never knew what love meant until I met you.
You are my first love and my only love
You are my soul mate.
You will be both my teacher and my student
and together we will grow to become better human beings.

Every day is full of choices.
and today I choose you to be my wife/husband.
From this day on, I promise to love you,
to be open and honest,
to respect you,
to support you,
to always stand by your side,
to accept and understand who you are,
to be your faithful husband/wife,
to be a comfort and safe haven in your life,
to grow as individuals and as companions.

Our love is a true love, the kind of love that will span
the ages. We will not part in life and we will not part
in death. I pledge myself to you for all eternity.

Blessing: A PART OF SPIRITUAL AND GROOM AT THE IT FELT SO SPECIAL AND I THOUGHT JOHN DID A SUPER JOB. IN INDIA, WHERE THE FRAGRANCE OF FLOWERS IN THE FORM OF INCENSE IS DEEPLY LIFE, THE BRIDE'S BROTHER TRADITIONALLY SPRINKLES FLOWER PETALS ON THE BRIDE CLOSING OF THE WEDDING. THIS WAS ANOTHER FAVORITE PART OF THE CEREMONY TO ME—

Christine's album successfully reflects the interesting aspects of her self-styled wedding. Note how the journaling, photos and creative cropping on the scrapbook page at right work in unison to depict an Indian wedding custom which Christine and Nicholas incorporated into their ceremony.

TO HAVE and TO HOLD.

Believe

The two of you seem to make each other better... really a beautiful thing to see. Respect each other & don't ever lose the ability to laugh at yourself and each other (my secret to a happy marriage).

Dad

I DO!

NICK AND I DECIDED TO WRITE OUR OWN WEDDING VOWS. IT WAS A CREATIVE, CHALLENGING AND ULTIMATELY REWARDING UNDERTAKING. NICK AND I WROTE OUR OWN VOWS SEPARATELY, THEN CAME TOGETHER FOR THE FINAL VERSION. OUR VOWS EXPRESS OUR OWN STORY OF PROMISES THAT WE CONTINUE TO LIVE BY. WHAT A GREAT EXPERIENCE!

Wedding portraits are revered for their historic significance to generations past, present and future. Formal portraits can be simply enhanced or elaborately embellished without taking attention away from the portraits. Here are some portrait pages that successfully showcase that moment in time when life together is new.

Wedding Prayers

ADD SILVER ACCENTS TO A SOFT LAYOUT

Use rose printed paper (Wübie) for page backgrounds. Mat photos and printed prayers with black paper. Adhere lacy heart stickers (Mrs. Grossman's) and silver photo corners and embellishments (Mark Ent.).

Linda Gibbs, Kennewick, Washington

Mr. and Mrs. Joshua Batz
May 16, 1998

Wedding Wreath

FRAME PHOTO WITH SAGE LEAVES AND FLOWERS

Photocopy the leaf pattern below to make this wedding wreath.

Mat photo behind 6½" hand-cut cream oval frame; double mat with handmade paper. To create the wreath frame, cut a ⅛" brown oval ring. Cut sage leaves using pattern. Score down the middle of each leaf using an embossing stylus and fold slightly to add dimension. Layer oval ring and leaves around photo. For each flower, punch three small white hearts for petals and a ⅛" yellow circle for the center. Lightly roll petal edges around a pencil; adhere.
Page inspired by Judy Anderson

Tom and Jan Cramer
August 1987

ON THIS OUR
WEDDING
DAY
FEB 13, 1999

Edward and Stephanie (Banker) Hofmeister
September 21, 1996

Tom and Jan

WEAVE A RIBBON FRAME

(UPPER FAR LEFT) Cut a 6" pink square and 7½ x 9" mint rectangle for photo mats. Emboss bow (Lasting Impressions) on top edge of mint mat. Emboss corners (Plaid Enterprises) on pink mat. Punch ⅛" holes in pink mat. Weave ¼" ribbon through holes and tie a bow. Hand-cut banner. Punch small white bells.

Marilyn Garner, San Diego, California

Doves and Hearts

ADD TEXTURE WITH PIERCED DIE CUTS

(UPPER LEFT) Mount photo on avocado background. Pierce hand-cut doves and hearts using a piercing tool, needle or pin. Layer shapes around photo.

Kristen Cruden Mason, Reston, Virginia

On This Our Wedding Day

ACCENT WITH PRINTED PAPER CUT OUTS

(LOWER FAR LEFT) Use black paper for background. Cut large tulips from printed paper (Frances Meyer) and mount on black background. Cut 8 x 9½" black rectangle; round top and cut out inside to form photo frame. Mount photo behind frame; mat arch on white paper and round top. Adhere tulip (Frances Meyer) and title (Mrs. Grossman's) stickers.

Bobbi Clarke, Middleburg, Florida

Edward and Stephanie

FRAME WITH INTRICATE DIE CUTS

(LOWER LEFT) Mount portrait beneath die-cut frame (Gina Bear). Mount die-cut leaves (Ellison) in corners. Use deckle scissors to trim printed title and mat.

Stephanie Hofmeister, Coronado, California

Wedding Silhouette

PROFILE THE BRIDE AND GROOM

Stephanie Hofmeister, Coronado, California

PAPER SILHOUETTES

Here's a simple way to create a silhouette portrait like the one shown above.

1. *Photocopy and enlarge a profiled photo of the bride and groom. Place yellow carbon paper (Saral Paper Corp.) and then black paper under the photocopy and trace outline of bride and groom with pencil.*
2. *Cut out the bride and groom silhouette. Punch ¹⁄₁₆" holes along bottom of bridal gown for lacy effect.*

Alternative methods: Cut out enlarged photocopy as template and trace with pencil on black paper or lay photocopy on black paper and cut out together.

With This Ring
I Thee Wed

CIRCLE CUT A QUILT DESIGN

Use printed paper (MiniGraphics) for page background. Use circle cutter to cut six 6½" circles—three rose and three purple. Cut out 5½" circles inside each circle to form the wedding rings. Intertwine two purple and two rose rings as shown, slitting each ring so they can be overlapped. Cut remaining rings into sections and arrange as shown. Crop photos and printed paper to fill the centers of each ring. Adhere ring and heart stickers (Frances Meyer).

Bobbi Clarke, Middleburg, Florida

Wedding Ring Quilt

COLOR COPY A TREASURED GIFT

The portrait frame was made by color copying and reducing a quilt square sewn with traditional French fabrics. Duplicate the idea using a quilt square from a wedding ring quilt or any quilt pattern that can be adapted as a photo frame. As an alternative, piece a paper quilt using a quilt pattern and printed papers.

Marie Dominique-Giraud, Lyons, France

Our Love

MAKE A WEDDING KALEIDOSCOPE

Mount forest green paper on black background. Follow directions at right to create photo kaleidoscope; trim to frame photo and mount. Mat diamond-shaped photo on black; mount in center. Journal around photo kaleidoscope; attach title.

Jennifer Blackham
West Jordan, Utah

PHOTO KALEIDOSCOPES

Photo Kaleidoscopes™ are made by using multiples of both the original photo and the reversed (or mirrored) image of the photo. Cutting these photos on an angle and piecing them together again will give you a dramatic kaleidoscopic design. For best results, select a photo that has vivid colors, good light quality and lots of activity, repetitive patterns or intersecting lines. For more on creating photo kaleidoscopes, see *Memory Makers Photo Kaleidoscopes*™. (See page 125 for more information.)

1. *For an 8½ x 11" page, start with four regular and four reversed image (made by photo lab, printed from flipped negative) photos. Place a clear, 45° triangle on one photo to determine cutting lines. Move it around until the part of the picture you wish to use is visible beneath the triangle. Find three distinct reference points on the photo which fall along the edges of the triangle. You will cut through these exact points on each original and on each reversed image photo.*

2. *Line up your triangle to match the three pre-selected reference points on each photo. With a craft knife, cut the photo using your triangle as the straight edge. Repeat exact cut on the seven remaining photos.*

3. *Using one cut piece from a regular photo and one from a reversed image photo, place the cut sides together, matching them into mirror-imaged pairs along your pre-determined reference points. Secure with removable tape. Repeat with all pairs of photos; assemble into page border matching all reference points. Trim center opening to frame photo; mount.*

Christine and David

ARRANGE A FLORAL SWAG

Use white page for background. Emboss two
vertical lines as shown on page with a wave
edge stencil and a straight stencil. Mat photo
with white embossed frame and colored paper.
(White frame shown is an embossed wedding
invitation.) Freehand cut flowers, buds and
leaves for floral swag. Draw stems and write
title with thin green pen.

Bev Klassen
Rosedale, British Columbia, Canada

Wedding Roses

USE A STENCIL TO PIECE BRIGHT FLOWERS

Trim four ¼" light blue strips along one
edge with deckle scissors. Mount strips
along page edges. Cut photos into 4½"
circles. Freehand cut curved flower stems.
Use birch leaf punch for leaves. Use rose
stencil (C-Thru Ruler Co.) to cut royal blue
pieces for each rose. Mount pieces on light
blue paper and cut out each flower.

Eileen Ruscetta, Westminster, Colorado

Jaime and C.J.

PUNCH LACY ACCENTS

Mount 8½ x 11" ivory sheet on left side of black scrapbook page (Creative Memories). Layer medium daisy, small daisy and mini heart punches for daisy border. Quadruple mat oval photo, invitation and marriage prayer. Add small and mini heart punches and ribbon to invitation. Trim the second oval mat with Victorian scissors and punch ¹⁄₁₆" holes. Mount negative pieces from scroll border punch for lace effect around photo and invitation. Mount daisy sticker (Mrs. Grossman's) over two scroll pieces.

Laurie Nelson Capener
Providence, Utah

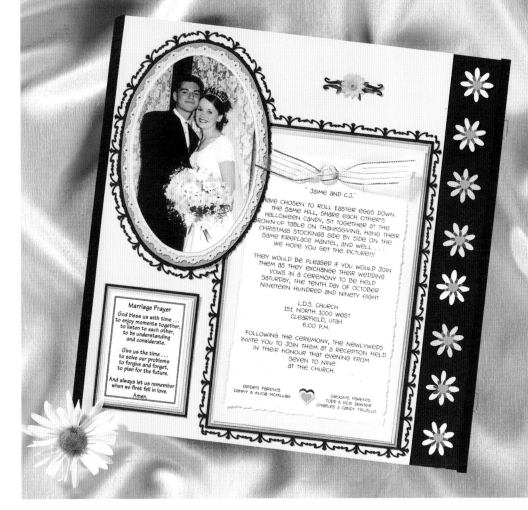

Always a Bridesmaid

LEARN A NEW LETTERING STYLE

Mat and layer photos on cloud paper (Geographics). Write title using lettering from book *LMNOP* (Cut-It-Up).

Holle Wiktorek
Clarksville, Tennessee

Heat embossed designs have a raised and shiny surface made by sprinkling embossing powder over a freshly stamped image, tapping off the excess and applying heat. The powder melts and forms a permanent bond to the ink, creating an embossed look.

To heat emboss a design, you must use a pigment stamping ink. Because pigment ink dries slowly, you can stamp several images before you sprinkle all of them with embossing powder.

Embossing powders are available in a variety of colors and styles. Opaque embossing powders completely cover the ink with the color of the powder, so you can use any ink color. For example, any ink embossed with gold powder turns gold. In contrast, clear embossing powders let the ink color show through. Other powders add special effects to the ink color such as pearl, sparkle or iridescent.

To heat emboss a stamped image, follow the steps below. Be sure to keep your photos away from the heat gun or other heat source.

From every human being there rises a light that reaches straight to heaven, and when two souls that are destined to be together find each other, the streams of light flow together, and a single, brighter light goes forth from that united being.

Love

EMBOSS FANCY LETTERS

Draw line border around page edges. Use scallop stencil (StenSource) to heat emboss scalloped edges of 11" ivory square. Trim around scallops and lightly color in. Stamp letters (Personal Stamp Exchange) and heat emboss using green verdigris embossing powder. Mat letters and photos. Use hearts and flowers border punch to embellish mat for rectangular photo, fancy scissors to trim oval photo. Adhere photos and letters; journal.

Joyce Schweitzer
Greensboro, North Carolina

1. Stamp the image with clear pigment ink. Liberally cover the design with embossing powder.
2. Tap off the excess, using folded paper to return extra powder to the container. Sweep away any tiny bits of powder with a soft brush.
3. Apply heat with a heat gun until the ink "rises and shines." You can also use a pre-warmed heat source such as a toaster or hot plate.

Morning Glories

INSPIRATION FROM THE BRIDAL BOUQUET

Draw purple double line border on purple background. Stamp purple morning glories (Personal Stamp Exchange) on lavender paper, heat emboss with clear embossing powder, and color in with markers. Cut out stamped designs and mount on 8¼ x 10¼" lavender rectangle frame. Triple mat photo using gold paper and the stamped rectangle frame.

Joyce Schweitzer, Greensboro, North Carolina

BASIC STAMPING

1. Choose the appropriate stamping ink.
Although the variety of labels and brands can be confusing, most stamping inks fall into two categories—pigments and dyes. Pigment inks are fade resistant but usually not waterproof. Because they take longer to dry, pigment inks are best suited for heat embossing (see page 74). Because dye inks in general tend to fade, use only dye ink pads specifically labeled acid-free, waterproof, permanent and fade-resistant. The advantage of a waterproof ink is that you can color in a design without smearing the ink.

2. Apply ink to the stamp.
Gently press the stamp on the pad or, if you prefer, tap the pad on the stamp. Take care to not over-ink. To see if the image is evenly colored, hold the stamp at an angle. If you see a dry spot, tap a little more.

3. Stamp the image on paper.
If you are using dye ink, "huff" hot air onto the design immediately before you stamp to remoisten the ink. When you press the stamp on paper, do not rock or wiggle, or the image might be blurry. The pressure required depends upon the size of the stamp and intricacy of the design, so always practice first on scrap paper.

Happy Bride

ASSEMBLE A PRESSED FLOWER GARLAND

Layer pressed flowers (see page 57) at top of page. Mount portrait with photo corners on printed paper. Trim corners of mat with round corner edger (Fiskars).

Heather Spurlock, Salt Lake City, Utah

Wedding Belles

CREATE CUT-OUT LETTERS OF PRINTED PAPER

Mat 8⅜" and 11⅜" squares of printed paper (Hot Off The Press) with cream paper. Double mat partially silhouetted photo. Cut letters for title using template (C-Thru Ruler Co.) and printed paper; mat with cream paper and trim outer edges. Journal with opaque purple pen.

Shauna Immel, Beaverton, Oregon

Wedding Gown

CHRONICLE THE MAKING OF A GOWN

(RIGHT) Trim ½" strips of blue paper with decorative scissors. Mount strips along edges of fern paper. Silhouette and mat photos; layer over journaling. Cut and mat banners for page title.

Donna Pittard, Kingwood, Texas

Special Tribute

Use a wavy ruler to draw lines ¼" apart on burgundy and light rose paper. Cut out wavy strips and intertwine along page border. Accent border, corner-rounded and silhouetted photos and trimmed and matted journaling with rose stickers (The Gifted Line).

Eileen Ruscetta, Westminster, Colorado

...d, the wedding gown of your dreams!

Detail of the back of the gown & train.

I started beading the lace on 5-1-97 and finished the gown and veil on 7-16-97

The gown had a beautiful detachable train, and boy was it heavy!

I also beaded matching shoes & her keepsake album.

...of the front of ...wn. All of the lace & ...dded 11 lbs. to the dress

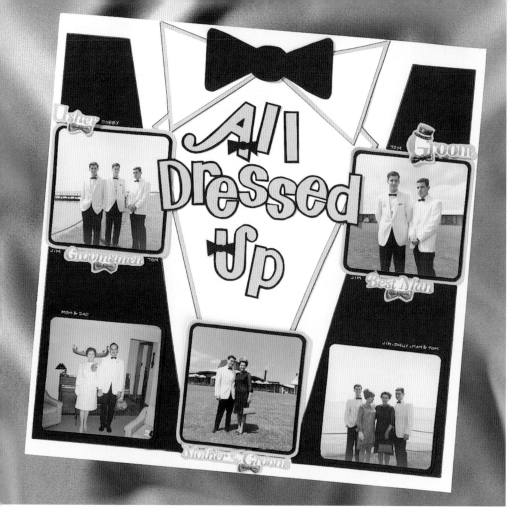

All Dressed Up

TAILOR A TUXEDO PAGE

For jacket lapels, cut black triangular shapes 4¼" wide at the bottom and 1¾" wide at the top, adhere and outline in black ink. Cut two triangles for white bow and kite shape for shirt front; mat with lavender paper. Double mat photos. Apply wedding stickers (NRN Designs). Use template (Pebbles In My Pocket) to cut and mat title letters. Freehand cut large and small bow ties.

Cynthia Castelluccio
Carrollton, Virginia

The Groom

IMITATE HIS TUX WITH PAPER

Use silver pen to draw bow ties and write title along border of black scrapbook page (Creative Memories). Cut 7" white square for tuxedo shirt. Vertically adhere 1¼ x 7" white strip down shirt front. Punch ¼" black circles for buttons. Mount photos. Cut white triangles for collar. Freehand cut black bow tie.

Lorna Dee Christensen, Corvallis, Oregon

ORIGINS OF COMMON WEDDING TRADITIONS

DRESS   *Ancient Greek and Roman brides wore white; not truly in vogue until mid-19th century wedding of Queen Victoria. Prior to that, "Sunday best" or a new dress that could be added to everyday wardrobe was worn.*

VEIL   *Symbol of purity and of the bride still being part of her father's house; also symbolizes bridal protection from evil spirits and would-be robbers.*

RINGS   *Ancient Egyptian symbol of eternity; worn on second finger of left hand because it was believed that a vein ran directly from that finger to the heart.*

VOWS   *For millenniums, brides have stood at the left of their groom when taking their vows to keep grooms' right hands free to fend off would-be marauders.*

KISS   *Symbolizes the first moment in time when bodies unite as husband and wife.*

TOSSING RICE   *For centuries, rice and other grains have been tossed at newlywed couples to grant them a large harvest of babies. Today's newlyweds also release doves or butterflies or have wedding guests blow tiny bubbles after the ceremony.*

BELLS AND HORNS   *Noise-making has been used to frighten away evil spirits for centuries. Clanging bells and blasting firearms have given way to today's honking of horns in motorcades.*

CAKE   *Ancient Rome; newlyweds fed each other with the first slice of wedding cake to pledge their fidelity by sharing food.*

BRIDAL BOUQUET AND GARTER TOSS   *14th- and 15th-century England; young males would dash at the bride, hoping to grab her garter for a trophy. Brides began to tear off their garters and throw them quickly. By the 18th century, the tradition had evolved into tossing the bridal bouquet, with the belief that whoever catches it will be the next to marry.*

The Groom's Men

STAMP SILVER SWIRL ACCENTS

Mat 4½ x 10" rectangles of printed cardstock with silver paper and mount on left and right sides of layout. Stamp and emboss silver swirls (Stampin' Up!) on 9⅜ x 7⅜" photo mat and title letters (Stampin' Up!) on left page. Layer photos with preprinted tuxedo (source unknown). Journal and draw line borders with silver pen.

Joyce Schweitzer, Greensboro, North Carolina

Bridal Portrait

WEAVE A FLORAL LATTICE

Layer ¼" mauve strips in a lattice pattern.
Stamp, color in and assemble bow photo
corners (J.D. Impressions). Double mat
photo and add black pen stitching.
Use stencil (Provo Craft) to cut banner.
Punch mini hearts to fill lattice. Use teardrop
pieces from tulips and hearts border punch
(All Night Media) for green leaves. Journal
and draw stitch lines with black pen.

Marilyn Garner, San Diego, California

Kristen's Bridesmaids

DOCUMENT THE BRIDESMAIDS'
RELATIONSHIPS WITH THE BRIDE

Use printed paper (Keeping Memories Alive)
for page background and oval photo mat.
Trim gold oval mats with decorative scissors.
For title, stamp and heat emboss gold frame
(All Night Media) on black paper. Mat frame
and typed journaling with gold paper.
Draw line border with gold pen.

Joyce Schweitzer, Greensboro, North Carolina

4 generations
bride: Marie Antoinette
flowergirl: Patrice Strama
Mom: Hilda Casanova
Antonia Morales-granny

Hertiage is more precious, with every passing day,
Traditions keep us close, in a very special way.

My Wedding Day
August 15, 1981

This picture is one of my favorites,
with four generations of my family. My
granny, mother, daughter and myself.
This is the last picture of the four of
us before granny died.
Granny was born in Puerto Rico, both
her parents were born in Spain, her
father was a Baron. Mama was born
in New York. Mama's father was born
in Puerto Rico. I was born in New York.
My father's parents were born in
Northern Italy and Sicily. Patti was
born in California.
Granny is a fabulous seamstress, she
can make any dress she sees. Granny
made Patti's beautiful gown and her
own dress. Patti use to call this dress
"her wedding dress".

BelINDclÓ INfES   JASON IMES

Four Generations

JOURNAL ON A WEDDING ROSE

Use printed paper (Keeping Memories
Alive) for page background. Trim corners
of portrait with Regal corner scissors
(Fiskars). Use journaling template
(Chatterbox) as template for rose.
Freehand cut stem and leaves.

Marie Valentino, Shelton, Washington

Flower Girl and
Ring Bearer

COLLECT WEDDING AUTOGRAPHS

Adhere ¾" blue strips around edges of
striped background. Punch and layer
medium daisies and tiny flowers on
background. Double mat photo and
autographs, mitering corners of paper
lace (Close To My Hearts/D.O.T.S.)
on photo mat.

Linda Gibbs, Kennewick, Washington

Paper Dolls

CRAFT WHIMSICAL NEWLYWEDS

Mount photos on beige background.
Dress doll die cuts (Accu-Cut) with
vellum paper (The Paper Co.) for
bride's veil and scallop punch (Family
Treasures) for groom's hair. Adhere
bouquet sticker (Frances Meyer).

Heather Spurlock, Salt Lake City, Utah

The Cortez Bunch

COMPOSE A MUSICAL TRIBUTE

Crop and mount photos. Write
song lyrics with thin black pen.
Adhere music note stickers
(Mrs. Grossman's).

Ann Cortez, Tehachapi, California

DESTINATION AND THEME WEDDINGS

Many couples choose to break with tradition by letting the nuptials reflect their individuality–through destination and theme weddings. These unique ceremonies run the gamut, from the romantic getaway ceremony in Fiji to the speedy flight to a Las Vegas chapel and from a winter wonderland wedding complete with sleigh ride to ceremonies heaped in western flair.

One thing is for sure. These celebrations have just the character and personality needed to create unique, unusual and unforgettable wedding scrapbook albums.

Sherry Harrison, Henderson, Nevada

Karen Greenberg, Winter Springs, Florida

POPULAR DESTINATION AND THEME WEDDINGS

Black and White
Christmas
Dawn of the New Millennium
Disneyland or Disney World
English Garden Party
European
Seaside or Maritime
Las Vegas
Medieval or Renaissance
Napa Valley Wine Country
Storybook or Fairy Tale
Victorian
Western
Winter
1920s Art Deco
1940s Big Band/Swing

Jennifer is not very comfortable with her own handwriting in her album, preferring instead to use "open" type fonts for journaling. These types of fonts allow her to use a craft knife to cut out the "open space" in the letters and mount printed paper or photo scraps underneath, creating an illuminated stencil effect.

Note the widespread use of creative photo cropping, which results in a contemporary alternative to standard, rectangular photos.

A Kiss to Build a Dream on

Let Them Eat

Cake

Jennifer's use of simple, colored card stock and sparse use of printed papers adds to the polished look of her page layouts.

Fire and Ice

Bride Side

25 July 1992
Garden Reception

Rex and Zada Norman
Wendy
Chris, Sandy & Connor
Jan & Gray
Derek and Shane
Marge and Lamar
Amy & Scott

Today's ethnic brides and grooms are creating celebrations that blend contemporary wedding customs with re-enactments of ceremonial traditions from their native lands. For example, a Japanese bride may wish to honor her family with a traditional Shinto wedding, complete with kimono and elaborate hair style. Then later, don a white wedding gown and cut cake at the reception.

The result, when compiled into a wedding scrapbook album, is a custom-made heritage lesson full of richness and meaning for your children's children.

Two Families Become One

MAKE AN HAWAIIAN WEDDING QUILT

Use cream-colored paper for background. Copy and enlarge hearts to use for pattern. Punch four purple triangles with slot punch (Family Treasures); adhere to page. Mat pink, cream, purple, pink and cream-colored papers; insert into corner slots. Add hand-cut green vine and two double-matted photos. Accent with hand-cut layered hearts and computer label (DJ Inkers). Draw pen-stroke stitching with black pen.

Robyn Hallsten, Torrance, California

Hawaiian Lei Bestowing

RE-CREATE ISLAND WEDDING TRADITION

Mount main photo on page. Circle cut two
3¾" and two 2¾" photos; mat on blue paper
trimmed with Victorian scissors (Fiskars).
Adhere photos. Accent with lei made of
punched small blue flowers and small green
hearts. Letter flowers in gold ink.

Carolyn Pearl, Honolulu, Hawaii

Hawaiian Groom's Page

BUILD A CATHEDRAL WINDOW AND VINE

Photocopy and enlarge page shown to make a
pattern for the cathedral window. Crop photos
to fit each window pane; assemble on page.
Accent with large punched hearts and hand-cut
leaves. Draw vine with black pen. Accent with
border (Mrs. Grossman's) and church stickers
(Creative Memories) as shown.

Arlene Santos, Mililani, Hawaii

Just Married

Mount 2" strips of red (the color of
prosperity and good tidings in Hindu
weddings) paper across top and bottom
of pages. Corner round punch photos
and mount. Hand-cut paper dolls.
Dress dolls in traditional Indian "saree"
and "dhoti and khurta"; adhere. Accent
with stickers (Creative Memories, Mrs.
Grossman's Whispers Design Lines) and
white punched mini flowers.

Aruna Sivakumar, Cincinnati, Ohio

CULTURAL TRADITIONS

CHINESE
*Red bouquet (color of love, luck and joy in Old
China); bed linens changed to red (symbolizes setting
up bridal bed); traditional Chinese wedding banquet;
retreating line after banquet as opposed to having
receiving line after wedding ceremony.*

ITALIAN
*Groom carries a piece of iron (tocca ferro) in his
pocket to ward off evil spirits; torn bridal veil (good
luck); buste: bride carries a satin bag (laborsa) in
which guests place gifts of money; couple shatters a
glass at end of day (pieces represent number of years
of wedded bliss); candy-covered almonds (confetti) tied
in mesh bags tossed at the newlyweds (wishes for
many children).*

JAPANESE
*Shinto-style ceremony held at a shrine in
traditional kimono attire; sake (rice
wine) is drunk during ceremony
(symbolizes couple's purification,
merging of two families).*

SCOTTISH
*Bride wears a tartan sash over her dress in a plaid
that matches the groom's (symbolizes clan she is
marrying into); Scottish shortbread broken over bride's
head (good luck); Church of Scotland marriage vows in
Gaelic and English; Celtic knotwork wedding rings
(engraved with "Tha gaol agam ort" meaning "I love
you"); bagpipes play "Highland Wedding."*

Debra and Mark
CELEBRATE JEWISH HERITAGE WITH CREATIVE CROPPING

Mount invitation and menu on textured paper background. Use black and gold paper, corner rounder and starburst lace edge punch (Family Treasures) to crop and mat rectangular photos; layer next to memorabilia. Silhouette remaining photos; layer with die cuts (Accu-Cut) along bottom of page. Punch silver lovebirds (Family Treasures); mount in upper right corner of photo. Cut out silver diamond for ring die cut. Adhere stickers (Mrs. Grossman's).

Eve Lowey
Huntington Beach, California

Jumping the Broom
SHOWCASE AFRICAN-AMERICAN SLAVE WEDDING TRADITION

Make a broom die cut with hand-cut handle and jumbo wave scissors (Family Treasures) straw. Attach purple bows (represents prayers of mothers, grandmothers and great-grandmothers) and stickers (Mrs. Grossman's); adhere broom to page. Oval crop photos, double mat with rice (The Paper Co.) and gold paper trimmed with deckle scissors (Family Treasures); mount two photos using foam spacers to give added dimension. Add journaling; attach label.

Sekile Nzinga-Johnson
Lanham, Maryland

Connie Mieden Doyle to Anthony Cox

MARRIED JULY 29, 1999 GIRLEY, KELLS, COUNTY MEATH, IRELAND

While green is considered unlucky at Irish weddings, Connie's choice of emerald green, black and white backgrounds add just the right touch of drama to her cultural wedding album.

Rubber stamps (Highlander Celtic and Appalachian Art Stamps), hand-painted borders and art, copied from The Book of Kells, and hand-drawn Celtic lettering create a strong sense of medieval Irish tradition.

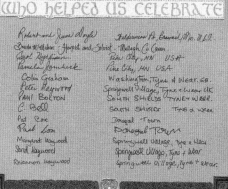

Weddings IN IRELAND TAKE from early morning to early morning. from the church to the reception and then to the lounge the celebrations continue. After pints are poured and more pints are poured, the 'craic' is good. Stories are told of past times by families and friends.

Handwritten guest list:

Carol Anne Walsh, Mahonstown Lodge, Kells
Pauline Duncan, Glasgow Scotland
Sheedarka Turin Italia
Barry Walsh Mahonstown Lodge Kells
Jehn + Linda O'Halleral, Beaconsfield, UK
David Mayor Jarrow England
JoAnn Amey Athens Ohio
Herb Amey Athens Ohio
May Price Marcarmillen
Kathleen Smith Kells
John Smith Kells
Linda Wilson Sunderland UK
Andrew Wilson
Alisdair Wilson
Robin Duncan
Paul + Loretta Brogan
Carol Patterson Athens OH

Connie's journaling of historical facts about Irish weddings works well with her photos in conveying Old World charm on her scrapbook pages.

BEFORE LONG A SONG BREAKS OUT AND EVERYONE SOON JOINS IN.

To Have and To Hold . . . .

Donna & Scott

Wedding Reception

JOIN US AS WE TOAST

THE FUTURE,

CUT THE CAKE

AND CELEBRATE

WITH FRIENDS

AND FAMILY...

Your wedding reception sets the mood of your celebration. Since the Middle Ages, receptions have been a time to relax and feast with family and friends. A time for toasting the future, cutting the cake and dancing the night away. It's the perfect ending to a perfect wedding.

Candid moments abound and you will want to get all of the photos you can from your professional photographer and your guests. Saving memorabilia such as table confetti, favors, and menus will make your reception pages more endearing with the passage of time.

TO HAVE AND TO HOLD
DONNA PITTARD
KINGWOOD, TEXAS
(SEE PAGE 124)

Sending All Our Love

Mount lavender paper at an angle across white background. Pen stitch around paper in black. Adhere bubble bottle and wand die cuts (Treasured Keepsakes) and circles cut from bubble paper (Hot Off The Press). Mat photo behind embossed frame (Keeping Memories Alive). Double mat frame with lavender and navy paper; adhere. Adhere envelope and insert wedding favor seed packet. Accent page and envelope with stickers (Mrs. Grossman's, Printworks).

Cyndi Malefyt, Grand Rapids, Michigan

A Key Toast

Following traditional toasts made to the bride and groom's health and happiness at Lisa and Rod's wedding reception, Lisa's mother, Eileen, broke tradition by offering a toast to welcome Rod into the family. But this toast had a twist.

Prior to the reception, keys were placed on the guests' tables with tiny notes that read, "Please hold onto this key until the mother of the bride gives her toast. Listen for her directions. She'll let you know what you need to do with your key. Please keep this under wraps...it is a surprise for Lisa and Rod."

Eileen's special toast included the request "for anyone who has dated Lisa in the past, please return my house key at this time."

Lisa and Rod were great sports as dozens of men jokingly tossed house keys into a stainless steel bowl that had been placed at Lisa's feet. It was a key toast that will go down in the record books as one of the funniest toasts ever made at a wedding reception.

Eileen Ruscetta, Westminster, Colorado

Tatia and Josh

CONSTRUCT A MINI POP-UP

Cut around flower petals of printed frame (Sonburn).
Slip photo beneath cut-out petals. Mount photo on
printed paper (Hallmark). Mat again with lavender
paper. Assemble pop-up using reception card as
described below. Adhere bow and page title.

Judy Anderson, Blue Springs, Missouri

POP-UP CARD

*For this mini pop-up, triple accordion fold a strip of
paper, mount inside the reception card, and adhere
silhouetted photos. Follow the complete steps below.*

1. *Cut a 4½ x 8"
rectangle of white
paper. Starting at the
4½" end, accordion fold
the strip like a fan using
1" folds. You will make
7 folds in all. Adhere each end
flush to the inside of the card
so that three folds stand up.*

2. *Print journaling and trim edges
with decorative scissors. Mount inside
card. Select photos for the pop-up. Silhouette crop
portions of each photo to fit inside the card.*

3. *Adhere the silhouetted photos to each of the three
folds of the pop-up card, mounting the shorter photos
in the front.*

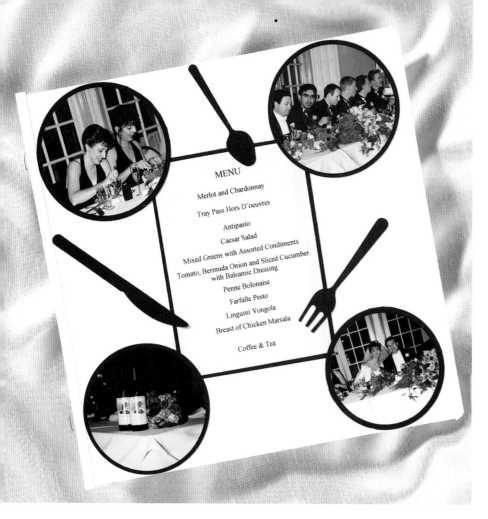

MENU

Merlot and Chardonnay

Tray Pass Hors D'oeuvres

Antipasto

Caesar Salad

Mixed Greens with Assorted Condiments

Tomato, Bermuda Onion and Sliced Cucumber
with Balsamic Dressing

Penne Bolonaise

Farfalle Pesto

Linguini Vongola

Breast of Chicken Marsala

Coffee & Tea

Reception Menu

SAVOR DELICIOUS MEMORIES

Mat menu with black paper. Circle cut photos and black mats. Adhere knife, fork and spoon die cuts (Creative Memories).

Renée Schwartz, Seal Beach, California

Wedding Reception

POP OPEN A BUBBLY BOTTLE

Trim rectangle for background with decorative scissors. Freehand cut black champagne bottle and draw details with silver pen. Use circle cutter and small circle punch to cut "bubbles" from photos and black paper. Layer elements with rectangular photos.

Terri Paul, Tallahassee, Florida

Todd teaches Peggy, Davette + Lorraine
the proper way to drink tequilia

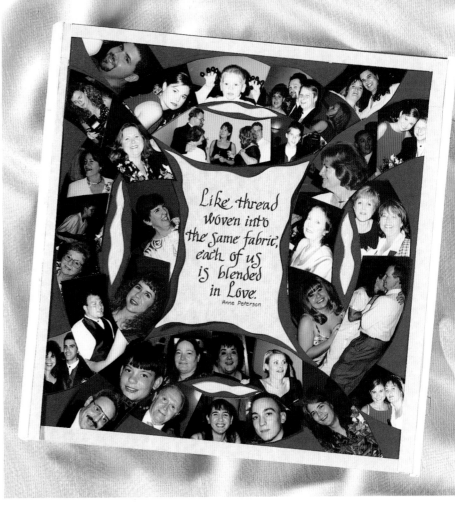

Blended in Love

MAKE A WEDDING RING QUILT OF GUESTS

Start with a 12" sheet of evergreen paper.
Pencil a 7" circle in the center. Cut out
the circle, freehanding a wavy edge.
Mount light green parchment beneath
the cut-out hole. Mount narrow strips
of parchment around page edges. For
curved evergreen arches, use a 10" circle
template to cut two circles with a wavy
edge. Cut out the insides of these circles
so the rings are about 2" wide. Cut each
circle in half. Trim and arrange arches as
shown. Piece photos on each arch.

Kathleen Taylor
Kearneysville, West Virginia

The Dance

A SCENE WITH A MUSICAL BACKGROUND

Mount music paper (source unknown)
diagonally on page. Mount photo
with corners. Adhere preprinted rose
die cut (The Family Archives).
Journal with gold pen.

Jennifer Lloyd
Pitt Meadows, British Columbia, Canada

Wedding Cake

CREATE A CUT-OUT PAGE IN SHAPE OF CAKE

Mat photos with pink paper and trim with decorative scissors. On center page, cut "stair steps" to create cake shape; mount photos. Adhere rose (NRN Designs) and gold letter (Frances Meyer) stickers.

Kay Mitchell, Gainesville, Florida

The Garter

FOLD A LACY ACCENT

Draw and color line border. Fold paper lace (source unknown) to resemble a garter. Accent with flower sticker (Love Lace). Double mat photo using floral (Paper Patch) and plum paper.

Heather Spurlock, Salt Lake City, Utah

Bouquet Toss

LAYER PHOTOS FOR PERSPECTIVE

Use wavy ruler and green pen to outline
and color green ribbon border. Trim
corners of large photo and colored mat
using Regal corner scissors (Fiskars).
Silhouette bouquet photo. Punch small
shamrocks from photo scraps. Adhere
flower stickers (Creative Memories).
Journal and draw lines with purple pen.

Kathleen Phelan, Baltimore, Maryland

His Folks, Her Folks

COMBINE PAST WITH THE PRESENT

Trim photos with decorative scissors
and double mat. Write title and journal
with thin and thick black pens. Adhere
wedding stickers (Frances Meyer).

Kari Murphy, Olympia, Washington

First Dance

BUILD A POP-UP WEDDING ARCH

Assemble pop-up as explained below. Trim photo corners with corner rounder punch. Print title, trim with decorative scissors, mat, and round mat corners. Adhere ribbon and floral stickers (Mrs. Grossman's).

Michelle Sharp, Orlando, Florida

POP-UP PAGE

1. *Trace pop-up template (C-Thru Ruler Co.) onto sturdy paper. Cut out template using a craft knife, ruler and cutting mat. Score along fold lines.*

2. *Cut two 1¼ x 7" strips for left and right columns of arch. Cut an 8½ x 2½" strip for arch top, trimming top corners as shown. Assemble arch; mount the photo beneath. Fold arch and photo in half vertically; mount over pop-up base. Adhere dove die cuts (Ellison), ribbon and stickers (Mrs. Grossman's).*

3. *Adhere pop-up tabs to left and right pages of layout so that the assembly folds flat when the album is closed.*

Mark and Viola

LAYER PHOTOS TO CREATE A CAKE

Cut out inside of printed cake paper
(Gussie's Greetings) following cake
outlines. Trim photos to fit each layer.
Separate layers with white paper strips
trimmed with decorative scissors. Adhere
additional heart photos. Trim page edges
with decorative scissors and mount on
sage background.

Traci Johnson, Mesa, Arizona

WEDDING FAVOR BOXES

Stamp beautiful gift boxes for your reception.

BUTTERFLY BOX— *Stamp background of pyramidal gift
box (Magenta) in brown with bold ornament stamp
(Magenta). Stamp four butterflies (Magenta) onto
cardstock; emboss in gold. Color in butterflies with
lavender and dusty rose pens. Cut out butterflies
and curl lightly around a thick marker; glue one on
each side of the box. Fold box and tie a curly ribbon
at the top.*

FLOWER SPRIG BOX— *Rub white pigment on a pyramid
gift box. Stamp box sections in brown with sprig of
flowers, butterfly and ornament (Magenta). Fold box
and tie a curly ribbon at the top.*

Natalie Petrarca and Catherine Parent, Magenta Rubber Stamps

Anny's black and white wedding album is elegant and dramatic from the use of soft vellum and black pages. Vellum overlays, placed next to photos of the guests, contain guests' signatures and good tidings. Vellum doors, made to mimic the Mediterranean arched doors of the hotel where the wedding reception took place, open up to reveal photos from the couple's reception.

Embroidered and silk daisies give the album an unpretentious charm. And the unique touch of embellishments add to the clean, crisp and classic appearance of the pages.

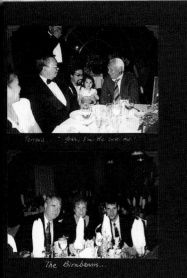

Terissa ... "Yeah, I'm the cutie one!"

The Birnbaums...

Life and Liberty

left to right; top to bottom
The bride & grooms mother-son
dance; dance with Lori Getty;
The "kiss"; Now and forever
father-daughter dance; K. with
our first dance "For the first time
Cindy & Jiji enjoying their dinner
(as much as they can!); Cindy with
her friends from Skyline College;
Diane doing her the mother-son
dance; Unforgettable
Anny with cousin Lisa

The next generation...

Dave,
Marilou,
& Sean Patrick

Sean loves his mommy too!

Jennifer with Lola & Lolo
Soriano.

Another unique aspect of
Anny's wedding album is that
she included clippings of all of
her sources of inspiration,
including her wedding gown
and nosegays of gardenias as
seen in a magazine.

Curt + Bran

Honeymoon

THE BOUQUET HAS BEEN

THROWN. THE CAKE HAS

BEEN CUT. THE GUESTS

HAVE ALL GONE HOME.

YOU'RE ALONE AT LAST.

It's the official start of your new life and your first vacation together. No matter how many vacations the two of you may take throughout your married life, there's only one honeymoon...and it's your idea of perfection.

Whether it's the sand between your toes, horseback riding in a national park or a European tour, it doesn't get any better than this. Record all of the your honeymoon's excitement by keeping a journal, taking lots of photos and collecting memorabilia (see our list on page 110) for some very sentimental scrapbook pages.

CURT AND BRANDY
DOLLY WOODWORTH
VIRGINIA BEACH, VIRGINIA
(SEE PAGE 124)

Our Honeymoon

SHOWCASE PICTURESQUE PHOTOS

Trim corners of bottom left photo using corner frame punch (Family Treasures). Mat center photo with oval frame (Keeping Memories Alive). Draw title letters from *ABCs of Creative Lettering* (EK Success).

Robyn LaCroix, Milford, New Hampshire

Shelley and Steve's Honeymoon Mishaps

Shelley and Steve's Cabo San Lucas honeymoon trouble began at 5:45 a.m. when Shelley realized their plane left at 6:00 a.m. A later flight was arranged and Shelley discovered that their original flight had returned because of technical problems. She had also forgotten to bring her pre-paid vacation vouchers along. It took $75 in phone calls from the plane to ensure that the newlyweds wouldn't have to ride a donkey from the airport and sleep beneath a borrowed sombrero.

Next, Shelley's sandals were stolen, she developed a bladder infection, a man in the swimming pool was reading a book on infectious diseases and their Mexican restaurant ran out of guacamole. In Mexico!

On the last day of their honeymoon, Shelley and Steve needed $11 in exit tax to leave Mexico but the banks had closed and phone lines were down. When they found an ATM machine, neither could remember their PIN number. They finally sold their only asset–a coupon for a dinner cruise–for $50. Instead of their romantic dinner cruise they ate cold scrambled eggs, and no one ever asked them for the exit tax!

Shelley and Steve were happy to get back home and start their new life together. Despite all of the pitfalls, they had a wonderful and memorable vacation and look back in hysteria on their honeymoon of mishaps.

Shelley Potter, Fairbanks, Alaska

Honey & Moon

PLAY WITH PICTURE WORDS

Freehand cut 7¼ x 11" honey jar, 6 x 4" white jar label and large crescent moon. Draw jar details and outline moon with gold pen. Mount moon on 8½ x 11" black paper. Mount photos and adhere bee and star stickers (Mrs. Grossman's). Draw dashed lines and journal with black pen.

Cathryn Good
Raleigh, North Carolina

Honeymoon Sweet

ACCENT WITH SIMPLE FLOWERS

Mat photos and printed title. Freehand cut circles for flowers and leaf shapes. Draw details with brown pen.

Jody Weber, Lafayette, Indiana

Aruba

Mount tan square on blue background. Cut title from photos using letter template (Close To My Heart/D.O.T.S.). Mat letters with aqua paper. Draw line borders with thin pen.

Joyce Schweitzer, Greensboro, North Carolina

Kaanapali at Sunset

SHOWCASE PANORAMA PHOTOS

Trim and layer panoramic photos on black background. Adhere palm tree die cuts (Ellison). Journal with white pen.

Allison Wagner, Foster City, California

TOP TEN MOST ROMANTIC HONEYMOON DESTINATIONS

Hawaii
Tahiti
Jamaica
Bermuda
St. Lucia
U.S. Virgin Islands
France
Italy
Fiji
Greece

Off to the Honeymoon

PACK A SUITCASE TO ACCENT OLDER PHOTOS

Mount 4" tan strip across top of page. Adhere suitcase die cut (Crafty Cutter) and luggage tag (Frances Meyer). Freehand cut pink hearts and "clothing" coming out of suitcase. Mat and cut out lowercase gold letter stickers (Making Memories). Use template to cut "Fat Cat" letters (Frances Meyer). Mat letters and pink hearts with gold paper. Double mat photos.

Cynthia Castelluccio, Carrollton, Virginia

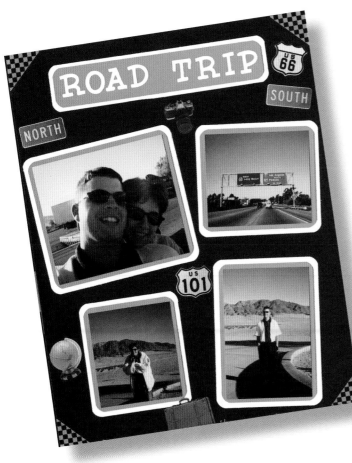

Road Trip

CROP PHOTOS INTO ROAD SIGNS

Double mat photos with green and white paper, trimming mat corners with corner rounder punch. Use white letter stickers (Frances Meyer) on green paper for title; mat with white paper. Layer travel-theme stickers (Frances Meyer) with photos on black background.

Holly Miller, Aiea, Hawaii

HONEYMOON PHOTO AND MEMORABILIA CHECKLIST

PHOTOS
- ☐ Honeymoon suite
- ☐ Newlyweds as photographed by other people
- ☐ Favorite restaurant
- ☐ Favorite romantic spot
- ☐ Favorite night spot
- ☐ Favorite sunset
- ☐ City skyline at night
- ☐ Underwater fun
- ☐ Architectural highlights
- ☐ Geographical highlights
- ☐ Historical landmarks
- ☐ People and culture unique to area
- ☐ New acquaintances met
- ☐ Lodging and restaurant signs

MEMORABILIA
- ☐ Maps
- ☐ Brochures
- ☐ Postcards
- ☐ Postage stamps related to area
- ☐ Event tickets
- ☐ Playbills
- ☐ Copy of passport
- ☐ Receipts
- ☐ Foreign coins/currency, if applicable
- ☐ Shells, sand, rocks unique to area
- ☐ Pressed flora/fauna unique to area

Our Honeymoon

SHOWCASE BROCHURE HEADLINES

Mount matted photo on page.
Add green paper strip "frame."
Crop titles and logos from
brochures and pamphlets; mount.

Kristen Cruden Mason
Reston, Virginia

Honeymoon Memories Shadow Box

CREATE A FUN, PERSONAL COLLAGE OF YOUR HONEYMOON MEMORIES

It's easy to make a shadow box display using your basic scrapbook supplies and your favorite scrapbooking techniques. The deep interior of a shadow box provides the perfect environment for mounting those beloved dimensional items and souvenirs collected on your honeymoon.

Add historical significance to your shadow box by including items from the honeymoon memorabilia list on the previous page. Before you know it, you'll have created a treasured time capsule that whisks you away to that romantic vacation as if it were yesterday.

SHADOW BOX TIPS

- Frame photos for added dimension prior to mounting in box.
- Self-adhesive foam spacers "lift" items from background for better shadowing.
- Mount photos with photo-safe mounting adhesives. Mount heavier items with beads of clear silicone, craft glue or a glue gun.
- Assume all memorabilia to be acidic and don't let them touch photos directly.
- Lay out the interior of your box completely before you glue items permanently in place.

Hyrum and Maria Jensen Olsen - Wedding Day
LDS Logan Temple, Utah - March 6, 1895

Heritage Weddings

CELEBRATING HOPE

FOR FUTURE

GENERATIONS BY

HONORING THE PAST....

Old wedding photos are a family treasure whose warm and inviting colors invoke sweet memories of bygone days. Heritage scrapbook pages can connect generations by unlocking the past and honoring the lives of those we hold dear.

Include as much narrative as you can on these precious scrapbook pages and add mementos to help capture the timelessness of the moment.

Take advantage of the many heirloom-related scrapbooking products on today's market. Or try a new technique to add elegance and richness to pages destined to become a lasting legacy.

HYRUM AND MARIA
LAURIE NELSON CAPENER
PROVIDENCE, UTAH
(SEE PAGE 124)

Debbie and Judie's Heritage Gift

In March of 1998, sisters Debbie and Judie began creating a heritage wedding album as a Christmas gift for their mother, a widow of nine years. "Nothing would make our mother happier than to see her old photos come to life again," says Debbie.

For six months, the two worked side by side with their three daughters—organizing, clipping and restoring old photos and memorabilia from a box that had been in their mother's basement for forty years. Among the buried treasures were an original wedding announcement, bulletin, napkin, newspaper clippings, old childhood photos and a dating scrapbook compiled by their father years ago. The sisters preserved as much of his original handwriting as possible for the new heritage album.

The album's title page explains the book to their mother and features an open locket with photos of Debbie and Judie's parents. The album's closing page features a closed locket with a bittersweet saying that is also inscribed on their father's tombstone. "We had so much fun working on the album that we could hardly wait for Christmas," says Debbie. "The joy we felt watching her open this gift was worth all of the work."

Debbie Streicher and Judie Mowery, Delaware, Ohio

A BRIEF HISTORY OF WEDDING PHOTOGRAPHY

For decades upon decades, couples have longed for wedding photographs that preserve the nostalgic memories of this most important family celebration.

Pioneer wedding photographers were limited to formal studio portraiture because of awkward photographic equipment. Portraits from these early days were somber due to long exposure times and usually featured only the bride and groom or sometimes just the bride.

By the late 1800s, enterprising photographers lugged their equipment to weddings, enabling other participants to be photographed. During the 1930s and 1940s, some studios sent photographers to the wedding for posed portraits and the occasional, experimental "candid action" shots.

The 1950s saw the advent of medium-format cameras and portable electronic strobes which allowed for full-service "candid wedding coverage." By the mid-1960s, colored photographs had become standard in the industry. Ultimately, the wedding photographers of the 1960s and 1970s are credited with unleashing the artistic freedom that set the precedent for today's highly creative, imaginative and dramatic wedding photography.

Marriage Certificate

DOCUMENT LONG-AGO WEDDING

Photocopy and reduce documents on pale pink paper. Double mat on corner punched (All Night Media) pink and black paper; adhere. Use wavy ruler (Creative Memories) and oval template to draw vines; freehand draw and color hearts and flowers. Adhere double matted photos trimmed with fancy scissors.

Linda Milligan, El Paso, Texas

Bride's Grandparents

DECORATIVE FRAMES PAY TRIBUTE

Use white corrugated paper (Snapz) for background. Mat photos with forest green paper and decorative frames (Gina Bear); mount. Double mat labels; adhere. Accent with ivy leaves cut from die-cut border (Ellison).

Stephanie Hofmeister, Coronado, California

WORKING WITH HISTORIC PHOTOS

For an archival-quality album environment:
- *Assume all memorabilia is acidic; never let photos and memorabilia touch.*
- *Use only acid- and lignin-free papers, photo-safe adhesives and pigment inks.*
- *Handle photos with care, avoiding direct light.*
- *Use nonpermanent mounting techniques (photo corners, sleeves, etc.) for easy removal for copying or restoration.*
- *Keep cropping to a minimum; background objects tell their own stories of place and time.*
- *Don't trim or hand-tint old photos; have reprints made first.*

QUILLING

Quilling involves rolling thin strips of paper into various shapes and arranging those shapes into a design. The standard width of quilling paper is ⅛", but wider and thinner sizes are available. Besides quilling paper, you'll need glue and a slotted or needle tool. Various shapes are made by rolling paper around the tool.

ROLLING WITH A NEEDLE TOOL

1. *Cut off a strip of paper to the desired length.*
2. *Slightly moisten one end of the strip and place that end against your index finger. Position the needle tool on the end of the paper, and press the end of the paper around the tool with your thumb.*
3. *Roll the paper while holding the tool steady, keeping the strip's edges as even as possible.*

Wedding Party

QUILL THIN PAPER STRIPS INTO CLASSIC DESIGNS

Mat photo and title. Use quilling techniques to roll tight circles for flower centers, teardrops for flower petals and green leaves, small white marquis shapes for flower buds, and scrolls and v-scrolls for stems and leaves. Glue rolled designs together to form flower garland. Adhere designs to page using tiny drops of glue.

Amanda Wilson, Colorado Springs, Colorado

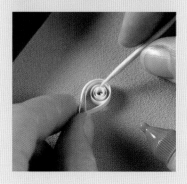

ROLLING VARIOUS SHAPES

TIGHT CIRCLE: *Roll, slip the tool from the roll's center, and hold it to keep it from unwinding. Glue the loose end of the paper to the side of the roll.*
LOOSE CIRCLE: *Roll, remove from tool, and let the coil loosen. Glue the loose end.*
TEARDROP: *Roll and glue a loose circle. Pinch one side of the circle to a point.*
MARQUIS: *Roll and glue a loose circle, and then pinch it on both ends.*
LOOSE SCROLL: *Roll one end, leaving the other end loose.*
V SCROLL: *Crease the strip at its center. Roll each end toward the outside.*

MEMORY-JOGGER LIST

*Journaling lends a human voice to heritage scrapbook pages. These helpful topics will
help you and family members reveal special details of their wedding day.*

- How and where the bride and groom met.
- The moment they knew they were in love.
- Tidbits from the days of courtship.
- Facts surrounding the proposal.
- Reactions of family members.
- National events of the era.
- Shower and bachelor/bachelorette party stories.
- Stories from rehearsal and rehearsal dinner.
- Why the wedding date was chosen.
- Facts about the wedding dress.
- Where the wedding was held.
- What the weather was like on the wedding day.
- Flowers chosen and why.

- The relationship of the best man/groomsmen, maid/matron of honor and bridesmaids to the bride and groom.
- Special vows, songs or poems at the ceremony.
- Funny or unusual stories about the planning and preparation of the wedding.
- Where and when the reception was held.
- Reception food, decorations and entertainment.
- Honeymoon destination and stories.

JANICE TOY
BLOOMINGDALE, ILLINOIS
(SEE PAGE 124)

September 3, 1934
Mr. and Mrs. Anthony A. Aurelia

Anthony and Marian

SHOWCASE HERITAGE PORTRAITS

Trim photo with corner rounder
punch and mat with lace paper
stickers (Mrs. Grossman's) and forest
green paper. Use script letter template
to write titles. Adhere flower and
ribbon stickers (Mrs. Grossman's).

Katherine Aurelia, Kokomo, Indiana

Mom's Wedding

SOFTEN WITH HANDMADE PAPER

Mount handmade paper on navy background. Cover photo corners with triangles of handmade paper. Add journaling.

Linda Strauss, Provo, Utah

KITE FOLD

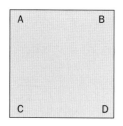

1. *Start with a square of paper.*

2. *With pattern side facing up, fold C and D to A and B, and crease.*

3. *Open flat, fold A and C to B and D, and crease.*

4. *Open flat and turn paper over with pattern side down.*

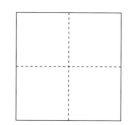

5. *Bring A to D, forming a triangle, and crease.*

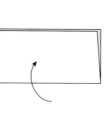 

6. *Open flat, fold C to B, forming a triangle, and crease.*

7. *Holding folded corners in either hand, push fingers toward center, forming a pocket opening, then move the corner in your left hand to the back and the corner in your right hand to the front, forming a layered triangle as shown.*

SCRAPBOOK PAPER FOLDING

With a few folds here, a few creases there and a little creativity, you can frame your memories in a whirl of three-dimensional paper splendor. For more on scrapbook paper folding, see Memory Makers Memory Folding™. (See page 125 for more information.)

While the wreath shown may look complicated, it is simply 16 folded squares layered in a circle. This particular folding technique, "the kite fold," is described on the previous page and below.

September 7, 1968

Kathleen Paula Kennedy

ASSEMBLY

Holding two pieces with closed points facing in the same direction, slide one piece into the space between the kite and flap of the other piece. Position the pieces so that the closed point of the inserted kite covers half of the wing of the other piece.

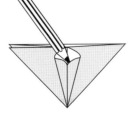

Kathleen Paula Kennedy

PAPER FOLDING FOR SCRAPBOOKS

Cut ¼" wide L-shaped slits in corners of black background. Mount printed paper (Hot Off The Press) beneath cut-out areas. Following the instructions, kite fold eight each of 2½" square silver and marbleized paper. Layer kite folds around 4½" circle as shown. Write titles with silver pen.

Amanda Wilson, Colorado Springs, Colorado

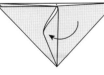

8. *Bring top right flap perpendicular to center fold.*

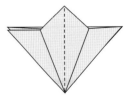

9. *Use a pencil to open the edges of raised flap.*

10. *Keeping center creases aligned, remove the pencil and press flat, creasing both sides of the new kite shape. Turn the piece over and repeat.*

Karen Ediger to Gordon Gerbrandt

MARRIED FEBRUARY 2, 1956 BUHLER, KANSAS

*P*am Klassen used styles of traditional paper cutting to create a heritage wedding album for her mother and father.

Her freehand designs integrate well with modified die cuts and stencil patterns to create a timeless, classic presentation on her album pages.

The Courtship

Tabor College

April 19, 1955 9:15 P.M. Tues. We decided to go steady.

May 24 - 8:30 - 12:00 PM I told her something.

July 26 0:05 I asked her to marry me - we're engaged!

LaVerne even bought my ring she told me.

Our first date: Sept. 15, 1954

1/1/56 - We've set our Wedding date for the 2nd of Feb.

Pam's consistent use of neutral and muted shades of paper throughout the album evoke memories of a simpler place in time, without taking attention away from the photos themselves.

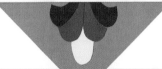

Pam's heritage wedding album was made in honor of her parents' 40th wedding anniversary. Because it was to be kept secret, the photos and memorabilia were borrowed without her parents' permission. As such, Pam didn't feel comfortable permanently mounting or trimming the photos. To solve her quandary, she used photo mounting corners so that each item could be easily removed at any given time.

Our Fairy Tale Romance

If you wish, use these convenient page titles to add an elegant finishing touch to your wedding scrapbook pages. Simply photocopy the lettering, scaled to the size you need, onto light-colored paper and color in with the pen of your choice.

I Do...

Love Takes Flight...

WE unite with joyful hearts

my answer was Yes!

Love Never Fails

1 CORINTHIANS 13:7-8

On the wings of
LOVE

Happily
Ever
After...

Now
&
Forever

Joined in friendship,
joined in love

happily
ever after

We unite with
joyful hearts

Our love unites us

title page
Wedding Mosaics
Larsja Peterson
Tyngsborough, Massachusetts
On a double page spread, use a 10" square grid as a guide. Trim photos to 2½" squares or 2½ x 5" rectangles. Arrange trimmed photos into the 10" square grid; adhere. Accent with stickers and borders (Mrs. Grossman's).

page 8
Jill and Randy
Mount 8½ x 11" dusty rose paper on sage green background. Frame photo with 8 x 10½" pale pink paper; mount on dusty rose paper. Punch sage green and dark green lg. birch leaves (Family Treasures). Hand-cut small slits in sage green leaves; layer over dark green leaves. To form dogwood petals, punch light pink and vellum lg. birch leaves. Adhere hand-cut strips of dark pink paper to light pink leaves; layer with vellum leaves. Trim away outer leaf edges and stems, cutting through all thicknesses. Snip into leaf tips with ¼" round hand punch. Assemble and adhere petals and leaves, allowing some to overlap photo. Accent with ⅛" round hand-punched yellow paper. Mat journaling on dusty rose paper; adhere.

page 9
Introduction
Photo of
Ron and Michele Gerbrandt

page 16
We're Engaged!
Use dark purple paper for background. Mount printed paper (Keeping Memories Alive) at an angle. Mount photos behind die cut frames (Keeping Memories Alive); adhere to page. Double mat photo with dark purple and navy blue, all trimmed with deckle edge scissors (Fiskars); adhere. Mount navy rectangle trimmed as above for journaling. Add engagement date in die cut title box (Keeping Memories Alive). Accent with rings (Frances Meyer) and hearts (Creative Memories) stickers.

page 17
Photo provided by Cathie Allan
St. Albert, Alberta, Canada

page 18
Engagement Window
Hand-cut window frame and sill from black paper. Adhere two rectangular "panes" from cloud paper (Hot Off The Press) and photo as shown. Punch the following shapes and adhere to window sill as shown: Lg. birch leaf, lg. flower, med. daisy, sm. spiral, sm. sun, sm. circle, sm. daisy, circle extension (Family Treasures).

page 30
Champagne Bridal Shower
Use lavender lace paper (Sonburn) for background. Mat invitation with blue paper and mount. Attach round photos. Accent with blue and purple

flowers from lg. flower punch and hand-cut green leaves.

page 31
Photo provided by
Eileen Ruscetta
Westminster, Colorado

page 40
Denise's Bachelorette Party
Mount hand-cut purple paper mountains to page. Crop photos to fit, mat if desired. Accent with memorabilia (postcard by RCS Co., Littleton, Colorado), cap stencil reduced (Provo Craft) and hand-cut, embossed (Lasting Impressions) vellum (The Paper Co.) veil.

page 41
Photo provided by
Eileen Ruscetta
Westminster, Colorado

page 46
Chad and Faith
Mount hand-drawn white paper at an angle on black page. Adhere photo and hand-cut roses and leaves. Accent with ¼" and ⅛" round hand-punched white paper.

page 47
Photo provided by
Laurie Jo Fehlberg
Rockford, Illinois

page 48
Calla Lilies
Pattern from calla lily sticker (Mrs. Grossman's). Cut out pieces

for flowers from photos and colored paper. Trim gold ring die cut (Accu-Cut) to look like prongs holding a diamond. Cut out "diamond" from silver ring die cut (Accu-Cut); mount beneath gold prongs. Adhere label. Slip lily stems through rings; adhere.

page 92
Donna and Scott
Mount 1" gold stripes vertically on sage green card stock. Adhere ¾" light sage green stripes to gold stripes. Cut hole in jumbo cake die cut (Ellison) for photo; adhere photo to back of die cut. Mount die cut and hand-cut gold platter atop stripes. Decorate cake with stickers (Mrs. Grossman's).

page 93
Photo provided by
Joyce Schweitzer
Greensboro, North Carolina

page 104
Curt and Brandy
Adhere beach paper (Wübie) to page. Mat photo with blue paper. Accent with dolphin (Accu-Cut), sea gull (Ellison) and starfish die cuts (Accu-Cut).

page 105
Design/photo provided by
Tammy Edinger
North Fort Myers, Florida

page 111
Photo provided by Lisa Wilson
Broomfield, Colorado

page 112
Hyrum and Maria
Adhere brown paper to page. Add ivory laser-cut paper (Gina Bear). Triple mount photo with brown and gold paper. Adhere photo and embellish with gold Victorian photo corners (Mark Ent.). Accent with bow border and micro mini bow punches (Family Treasures). Add gold Victorian border stickers (Mark Ent.).

page 113
Design/photo provided by
Doris Vogel
Wichita, Kansas

page 114
A Brief History of Wedding Photography
Private Collection, New York

page 117
Church
Hand-cut church and slit open door. Trim photos; adhere. Draw details with black pen.

page 128
Just Married
Design Lorna Dee Christensen
Corvalis, Oregon
Photo provided by
Mena Spodobalski
Sparks, Nevada

PROFESSIONAL PHOTOGRAPHERS

cover, page 67
Tatia and Joshua
Visual Images
400 E. Gregory
Kansas City, MO 64131

page 12-15
**Beginning Your Scrapbook,
Personal Design**
Diane Perry

page 18
Engagement Window
Cooper Photography
119 Valley NW
Grand Rapids, MI 49504

page 21
Engagement Portrait
Scott Hancock Photography
214 S. Main St.
Pleasant Grove, UT 84062

page 46
Chad and Faith
Sisson Studios
6813 Bland St.
Springfield, VA 22150

page 50
**Amy and Peter
Guests' Signatures Photo Mat**
Fotostudio August
A-5020 Salzburg
Paris-Lodron-Strasse 1
Austria

pages 59, 127
**I Now Pronounce You
Husband and Wife,
David and Mary**
Quigg Studio
8 Rolling Hills Dr.
Wichita, KS 67212

page 68
Edward and Stephanie
Hamilton's Photography
1716 Pepper Villa Dr.
El Cajon, CA 92021

page 68
Tom and Jan
Robert Oslie Photography
1509 Melody Lane
El Cajon, CA 92011

page 72
Wedding Roses
TCM Productions/Party Crashers
5978 S. Holly St.
Greenwood Village, CO 80111

page 76
Happy Bride
Newman Photography
4479 Highland Dr.
Salt Lake City, UT 84124

page 80
Kristen's Bridesmaids
Personality Portraits
White Plains, NC

page 82
Cortez Bunch
Scheibel Photography
PO Box 1138
Tehachapi, CA 93581

pages 90, 91
Connie Doyle to Anthony Cox
James Carney Photography
72 Flower Hill
Navan, County Meath, Ireland

page 98
Wedding Cake
Johnston Photography
1915 NW 13th St.
Gainesville, FL 32609

page 100
First Dance
Avalon Photography
1967 Rt. 27
Edison, NJ 08817

page 104
Curt and Brandy
Spectrum Photography, Inc.
941 General Stuart Dr.
Virginia Beach, VA 23454

BIBLIOGRAPHY

Blayney, Molly Dolan. *Wedded Bliss.* New York: Abbeville Press, 1992.
Brill, Mordecai; Halpin, Marlene; Genne, William. *Write Your Own Wedding Vows.* New Brunswick, NJ: New Century Publishers, 1985.
Diehn, Gwen. *Making Books That Fly, Fold, Wrap, Hide, Pop Up, Twist, and Turn.* Ashville, NC: Lark Books, 1998.
Jackson, Ellen. *Here Comes The Bride.* New York: Walker and Company, 1998.
Lee, Vera. *Something Old, Something New.* Naperville, IL: Sourcebooks, Inc., 1994.
Monteith, Ann. *The Business of Wedding Photography.* New York: Amphoto Books, 1996.
Ross, Pat. *I Thee Wed.* New York: Viking Penguin, 1991.
Sint, Steve. *Wedding Photography Art, Business, and Style.* New York: Silver Pixel Press, 1998.
Stewart, Arlene Hamilton. *A Bride's Book of Wedding Traditions.* New York: Hearst Books, 1995.

The following companies manufacture products featured on scrapbook pages in this book. Please check your local retailers to find these materials.

3L Corp. (847) 808-1140
1120 B Larkin Dr.
Wheeling, IL 60090

Accu-Cut Systems®
(800) 288-1670
PO Box 1053
Fremont, NE 68025

All Night Media®, Inc.
(800) 782-6733
PO Box 10607
San Rafael, CA 94912
(wholesale only)

Carl Mfg. of Hong Kong, Ltd.
(847) 956-0730
1862 S. Elmhurst Rd.
Mount Prospect, IL 60056

Cellotak (516) 431-7733
35 Alabama Ave.
Island Park, NY 11558

Chatterbox, Inc.
(888) 272-3010
PO Box 216
Star, ID 83669

Close to My Heart™ /D.O.T.S.
(888) 655-6552
738 E. Quality Dr.
American Fork, UT 84003

Crafty Cutter (805) 237-7833
179 Niblick Rd., #344
Paso Robles, CA 93446

Creative Memories®
(800) 468-9335
PO Box 1839,
St. Cloud, MN 56302

The C-Thru® Ruler Company
(800) 243-8419
PO Box 356
Bloomfield, CT 06002

Current®, Inc. (800) 848-2848
The Current Building
Colorado Springs, CO 80941

Cut-It-Up (530) 389-2233
32595 Frost Hill Pl.
Dutch Flat, CA 95714

Denami Design®
(253) 437-1626
PO Box 5617
Kent, WA 98064

Design Originals
(800) 877-7820
2425 Cullen St.
Ft. Worth, TX 76107-1411

DJ Inkers™ (800) 944-4680
PO Box 2462
Sandy, UT 84091

EK Success™
(800) 524-1349
125 Entin Rd.
Clifton, NJ 07014

Ellison® Craft & Design
(800) 253-2238
25862 Commercentre Dr.
Lake Forest, CA 92630-8804

The Family Archives™
(888) 662-6556
12456 Johnson St.
Mission, BC, Canada V2V 5X4

Family Treasures, Inc.
(800) 413-2645
24922 Anza Dr., Unit A
Valencia, CA 91355-1229

Fiskars®, Inc. (800) 950-0203
7811 W. Stewart Ave.
Wausau, WI 54401

Frances Meyer, Inc.®
(800) 372-6237
PO Box 3088
Savannah, GA 31402

Geographics, Inc.
PO Box 1750
Blaine, WA 98231

The Gifted Line®
(800) 533-7263
999 Canal Blvd.
Point Richmond, CA 94804

Gina Bear Ltd. (888) 888-4453
215 E. Foothills Pkwy., #H-1
Ft. Collins, CO 80525

Gussie's Greetings, Inc.
(972) 840-3545
2702 Industrial Ln., Suite L
Garland, TX 75041

Hallmark Cards, Inc.
(816) 274-3316
2501 McGee Drop., Suite 377
Kansas City, MO 64108

Heritage Handcrafts
(303) 683-0963
PO Box 261176
Littleton, CO 80163-1176

Hot Off The Press®, Inc.
(800) 227-9595
1250 N.W. Third
Canby, OR 97013

Hygloss Products, Inc.
(201) 458-1700
402 Broadway
Passaic, NJ 07055

JD Impressions
(559) 276-1633
PO Box 26895
Fresno, CA 93729-6895

K & Company (913) 685-1458
7441 W. 161st St.
Stilwell, KS 66085

Keeping Memories Alive
(800) 419-4949
PO Box 728
Spanish Fork, UT 84660-0768

Kolo®, Inc. (860) 547-0367
241 Asylum St., 6th Floor
Hartford, CT 06103

Lasting Impressions for Paper®, Inc.
(801) 298-1979
585 W. 2600 S. #A
Bountiful, UT 84010

Lee Valley Tools, Ltd.
(800) 871-8158
12 E. River St.
Ogdensburg, NY 13669

Lion Office Products
(800) 421-1848
401 W. Alondra Blvd.
Gardena, CA 90248

Love Lace Family, Ltd.
(719) 475-7100
2824 International Cir.
Colorado Springs, CO 80910

Magenta Art Rubber Stamps & Accessories
(800) 565-5254
351 rue Blain Mont-St-Hilaire
Quebec, J3H 3B4, Canada

Making Memories
(800) 286-5263
PO Box 1188
Centerville, UT 84014

Mark Enterprises
(800) 443-3430
1240 N. Red Gum
Anaheim, CA 92806

Marks of Distinction
(312) 335-9266
1030 West North Ave.
Chicago, IL 60622-2553

Memory Makers®
Memory Folding™ and Photo Kaleidoscopes™
(800) 366-6465
475 W. 115th Ave., #6
Denver, CO 80234

Microsoft Corp.
PO Box 72368
Roselle, IL 60172-9900

Minigraphics (800) 442-7035
2975 Exon Ave.
Cincinnati, OH 45341

MPR Associates®, Inc.
(800) 454-3331
529 Townsend, PO Box 7343
High Point, NC 27264

Mrs. Grossman's Paper Co.®
(800) 457-4570
3810 Cypress Dr.
Petaluma, CA 94954-5613

Northern Spy (530) 620-7430
PO Box 2335
Placerville, CA 95667

NRN Designs (800) 421-6958
5142 Argosy Ave.
Huntington Beach, CA 92649
(wholesale only)

Nu Century (435) 752-6590
955 Foothill Dr.
Providence, UT 84332

C.M. Offray & Son
(908) 879-4700
Route 24, Box 601
Chester, NJ 07930

The Paper Company®
(800) 426-8989
731 Fidaldo St.
Seattle, WA 98108

The Paper Patch®
(800) 397-2737
PO Box 414
Riverton, UT 84065
(wholesale only)

Pebbles In My Pocket®
(800) 438-8153
PO Box 1506
Orem, UT 84059-1506

Personal Stamp Exchange
(800) 782-6748
360 Sutton Pl.
Santa Rosa, CA 95407

Plaid Enterprises, Inc.
(770) 923-8200
PO Box 7600
Norcross, GA 30091-7600

Pressed Petals, Inc.
(800) 748-4656
35 West 200 North, PO Box 400
Richfield, UT 84701

PrintWorks (800) 854-6558
12403-B Slauson Ave., #B
Whittier, CA 90606

Provo Craft (800) 937-7686
285 E. 900 South
Provo, UT 84606

Puzzlemates (888) 595-2887
417 Associated Rd., #205
Brea, CA 92821

R.A. Lang (414) 646-2388
PO Box 64
Delafield, WI 53018

Ranger Industries®
(800) 244-2211
15 Park Rd.
Tinton Falls, NJ 07724

Royal Stationery
(800) 328-3856
PO Box 8240
Mankato, MN 56002-8240

Sakura of America
(800) 776-6257
30780 San Clemente St.
Hayward, CA 94544-7131

Sandylion Sticker Designs
(800) 387-4215
PO Box 1570
Buffalo, NY 14240-1570

Saral Paper Corp.
436-D Central Ave.
Bohemia, NY 11716

Snapz (714) 257-1111
2103 Brea Mall
Brea, CA 92821

Sonburn, Inc. (800) 527-7505
PO Box 167
Addison, TX 75001

Stampendous!®
(800) 869-0474
1240 N. Red Gum
Anaheim, CA 92806

Stampin' Up! (800) 782-6787
6746 Highway 89
Kanab, UT 84741

Stamping Station, Inc.
(801) 444-3828
249 S. Main
Layton, UT 84041

StenSource International, Inc.
(800) 642-9293
18971 Hess Ave.
Sonora, CA 95370
(wholesale only)

Stickopotamus®
(888) 270-4443
PO Box 1047
Clifton, NJ 07014

Sunrise Publications, Inc.
(800) 457-4045
PO Box 4699
Bloomington, IN 47402

Suzy's Zoo (858) 452-9401
9401 Waples St., Suite 150
San Diego, CA 92121

Treasured Keepsakes
(616) 530-8108
2030 Collingwood SW
Wyoming, MI 49509

Wübie Prints® (888) 256-0107
PO Box 1266
Sandy, UT 84091-1266
(wholesale only)

Unique and humorous departures.

Just Married

TAKE A RIDE IN A LIMO DIE CUT

Silhouette small wedding photos and mount in windows of limousine die cut (Ellison). Mount on black background. Adhere wedding stickers (Creative Memories).

Eileen Ruscetta, Westminster, Colorado

Golf Carts

SHOW THE GETAWAY VEHICLE

Mount photos on navy background. Journal and draw dots with silver pen.

Susan Seydel, Bonita, California

Harv's High-Flying Surprise

TELL A HELICOPTER STORY

Use corner punch (Carl Mfg.) to accent corners of rectangular mat and photos. Overlap circle photos and cut away overlapping areas. Mat circle photos and cut along right side of circles as shown. Silhouette photo of helicopter.

Bev Klassen
Rosedale, British Columbia, Canada

David and Mary

DRIVE AWAY IN A RED CONVERTIBLE

Trim mat for cloud photo with scallop scissors. Layer cloud with cityscape (Sonburn) and 3" wide blue paper road on cloud paper background (Frances Meyer). Draw road lines with thick white pen. Print banner, airplane and car clip art designs (Microsoft Publisher). Silhouette photo and mount behind car. Draw car exhaust with white pen.

Mary Lisenby, Wichita, Kansas

The Rivers Flow

SAIL IN A WEDDING ROWBOAT

Cut and layer brown hills, grass stickers (Mrs. Grossman's), blue river and green grass on cloud paper background (Design Originals). Tear blue strips for waves. Freehand cut tree trunk and branches. Punch large oak leaves from solid and printed (Keeping Memories Alive) papers. Freehand cut boat pieces to fit silhouette photo. Adhere die cuts (Crafty Cutter), rose (Printworks) and flower (Mrs. Grossman's) stickers. Add journaling.

Cyndi Malefyt
Grand Rapids, Michigan

Index

Not the end, just the start of a beautiful beginning...